THIS WILL MAKE

A MAN OF YOU

THIS WILL MAKE A MAN OF YOU

One Man's Search for Hemingway
and Manhood in a Changing World

Frank Miniter

Skyhorse Publishing

Skyhorse Publishing books may be purchased in bulk at special
discounts for sales promotion, corporate gifts, fund-raising, or educational
purposes. Special editions can also be created to specifications.
For details, contact the Special Sales Department, Skyhorse Publishing,
307 West 36th Street, 11th Floor, New York, NY 10018 or
info@skyhorsepublishing.com.

Skyhorse® and Skyhorse Publishing® are registered trademarks of
Skyhorse Publishing, Inc.®, a Delaware corporation.

Visit our website at www.skyhorsepublishing.com.

10 9 8 7 6 5 4 3 2 1

Library of Congress Cataloging-in-Publication Data is available on file.

Cover design by Tom Lau
Cover photo credit: iStockphoto

Print ISBN: 978-1-5107-1192-1
Ebook ISBN: 978-1-5107-1193-8

Printed in the United States of America

*To Ernest Hemingway for making the map
and to Juan Macho for guiding the way.*

Table of Contents

isn't apparent, one must be sought, as no rite of passage is real without enforcers and mythmakers. (Beware: a poor guide can ruin a grunt, student, or plebe.)

Now came the trials of running with bulls. The gauntlets in a rite of passage can be as ghastly as gloves filled with bullet ants, as grueling as boot camp, or as heart-pounding as running in a packed Spanish street with bulls; but whatever it requires, its challenges are there to prepare you for a metamorphosis that will only come if you endure the tests of mind, body, and spirit.

All real rites of passage have moral codes as their foundations, because without them the change isn't lasting. Perhaps this is why Hemingway was obsessed with his code. Whatever the case, the basis of Hemingway's code is surprising.

As you struggle and endure, you'll get the first taste of being what you've been pursuing. If you accept this, you'll be forever changed, still yourself but purified in a manly role.

If you pass the tests, you will be accepted among men of honor in a unit, team, company, firehouse, dojo, or, in my case, a peña. You are in a guarded society, a fraternity of men. But you also know the archetype you're trying to live up to will abandon you if you break the code, that to be all you can be, you must live up to something other than yourself. Of course it is much more than this, but that is why this is a book.

INTRODUCTION

A SHINING EXAMPLE OF A MAN

"Thank you," the old man said. He was too simple to wonder when he had attained humility. But he knew he had attained it and he knew it was not disgraceful and it carried no loss of true pride.

—Ernest Hemingway, *The Old Man and the Sea*

FLOYD PATTERSON, THE FORMER HEAVYWEIGHT champ, lowered the red punching mitts on his hands as he settled his brown, caring eyes into me. I knew he was choosing his words. I didn't know he was about to say something that would influence the rest of my life.

I was a fifteen-year-old, 130-pound kid who'd been training in the barn next to Floyd's home in New Paltz, New York, with dozens of other boys and a revolving cast of pro fighters for a year. I thought I was getting pretty good and wanted to know how good. So I'd paused between throwing a jab, right hand, left hook combination into those worn punching mitts and asked over the smashing clamor of the boxing gym if I had what it takes to be a champ.

Heavy bags were being pummeled around us. Their heavy chains were ringing. Someone was jumping rope, making its leather cord smack the barn wood planks under our feet. Another fighter was using his wrapped-up hands to make a speed bag go *bang, bang* then *bang, bang* as he shifted from left to right. Music was thumping Bruce Springsteen, and a round counter was ringing at one- and three-minute intervals.

Floyd's brow had furled under that lip of hair he always kept at the front of his head. He straightened his back while keeping his eyes locked in mine. I knew he'd adopted a lot of children and that he helped any who came to his gym. We all knew it didn't matter to him what our ethnicity was or whether someone had money or not. He just liked helping kids. So yeah, he was our role model, a giant among men.

Floyd knew this, so he carefully, a word at a time, said, "Only a really great fighter should make a go at being a professional boxer. Boxing destroys a lot of good fighters."

I was young, but not so cocky that I thought I was the next Sugar Ray Leonard. My expression must have shown this because Floyd pulled his punching mitt off in his armpit and put his hand on my shoulder. He then said just loud enough for me to hear in the smashing rhythm of that boxing gym, "I was younger than you when a teacher took me aside in reform school and told me to take a good long look at the people I thought were my pals. He said I should ask myself, really ask myself, if I wanted to be one of those kinds of guys, and not just right then, but all the way."

I glanced around the gym and back to Floyd's brown eyes as he said, "When I really looked at the guys in that reform school, I knew I didn't want to be one of those mugs, not all the way to prison. But when I got out and saw a fighter, I knew I wanted to be him all the way."

Floyd was a man of few words, and that was a mouthful of advice, so he slid his hand back into the punching mitt and raised the mitts up again.

As I again tried to perfect my technique, I knew I wanted to be like Floyd. He wasn't just a champ; in all the years I knew Floyd, I never saw him do an unmanly thing. He did everything with deliberate pride. He had the stoic strength and self-satisfaction of a man who'd done what he'd set out to do. There was no bully in him. There was no bravado. He was humble. He treated everyone with the same gentlemanly respect. If we stepped out of line, he'd set us straight, but never with anger in his eyes. He was our shining example of what a man should be.

My favorite Floyd story—and he liked to tell this—was when, late in his professional boxing career, a snide reporter asked him, "So Floyd, what's it like to be the heavyweight knocked down the most times?" Floyd politely replied, "Pretty good. Because I'm also the heavyweight champ who got up the most times."

That was the honorable nature of the man.

Still, as I took his advice and really looked around at the pros in the gym, I saw that I didn't want to be them, not all the way.

A few years later, as he signed a college recommendation letter for me, Floyd winked at me as he said, "Remember to ask yourself if you want to be one of those guys, and not sort of, but all the way. That will make a man of you. The man you really want to be."

He didn't say any more, but like any great teacher, he was handing me the keys to a lot more—if I'd only take them.

STEP 1

Chasing an Ideal

It is in the darkness of their eyes that men get lost.

—Black Elk, *Black Elk Speaks*

AT FORTY, I WAS IN a Paris café trying once again to answer Floyd Patterson's question. His advice to seek and deeply question our heroes in order to improve ourselves had made me a journalist and author, but I didn't know his simple advice to ask yourself "if you want to be one of those guys, and not sort of, but all the way" would become the key to answering a profound question modern society has been struggling with: What makes men?

This became clear as I used Floyd's advice to understand Ernest Hemingway. I went from the Paris cafés Hemingway wrote in to the streets of Pamplona, Spain, where men test their machismo with fighting bulls. At each step, I found that the answers to what happened to manliness, and therefore to what makes men, were in his story. This made sense, as Hemingway's iconic life, code, adventures, and fictional characters have been integral to every part of the last century's rise, decline, and fall of manliness. Actually, Hemingway has been loaded with so much that is right and wrong with manliness that following his footsteps quickly became both an intense rite of passage and an archeological dig for manliness.

Though, to be candid, I was off balance from the start.

I assumed I'd be looking into Les Deux Magots, a corner café in the Saint-Germain-des-Prés area of Paris that Hemingway frequented, to see what drew him to such cafés, but I saw that all the fashionable people seated around the small round tables on a bright July afternoon were facing the street.

They were seated in tan chairs under the café's green awning, because they wanted to see and be seen by the parade of Parisians on the walk and in the cars passing gently by on a summer afternoon. They were part of a living display begun generations before. The scene was coloring them with tender pastels and giving them timeless expressions and making their chatter as soft as jazz coming from an open window floors above. They looked like characters in the colorful Parisian prints sold to tourists along the Seine, though I supposed most of them wouldn't like to hear any such thing.

I should have known this, as this wasn't new. Hemingway said that in the 1920s many went to the popular cafés "to be seen publicly."[1] He went to them too, but he wrote in quiet,

---

[1] Ernest Hemingway, *A Moveable Feast,* Scribner's, New York, 1964.

neighborhood cafés where the crowds wouldn't find him during working hours. He separated the cafés into classes and treated them as their personalities dictated. To him, café life was central to why he said no other city was better arranged for a writer.

So yes, Hemingway's ghost seemed to be there among the white-linen tables and waiters in black bow ties, even though the times had changed and changed again. As I let myself become a part of that decadent and popular living art in that fashionable Paris café, I wondered how a man, an American man no less, a man who loved African safaris and fishing for trout in small streams and for marlin in the currents of the great blue ocean and who adored the loud and face-smashing scene in and around boxing rings, could also be in love with Paris café life.

I shook my head and grinned. The notion that those things are out of sync was taught to me by a society out of step with the well-rounded man. I'd come here to dissolve such nonsense. So I looked at all the decorative people and thought how silly it is that we've let the sophisticate slay the man in full—or at least banish him from polite society.

The late Michael Thomas Kelly (1957–2003), a writer and editor for the *Washington Post*, *The New Yorker*, *The Atlantic*, and more, actually blamed the king of cool, yeah Frank Sinatra himself, for today's misunderstanding of the Hemingway ideal.[2] Sinatra was perhaps America's first true pop idol of the Entertainment Age. Kelly wrote that "what Frank Sinatra projected was: cool." Before cool, there "was smart (as in the smart set). . . . The pre-Frank hip guy, the model

---

[2]Michael Kelly, *Things Worth Fighting For*, Penguin Press, New York, 2004.

of aesthetic and moral superiority to which men aspired, is the American male of the 1930s and 1940s. He is Humphrey Bogart in *The Big Sleep* or *Casablanca*." This old-school gentleman might have had the suave cynicism of Rhett Butler (Clarke Gable's character in *Gone with the Wind*), but deep down he adhered to the old values, which was why Butler finally joined the war even as the South was crumbling. This old-school man would patriotically go to war and believe, despite the messiness and gross immorality of war, that somehow he was fighting for something good, and so he was good. This pre-Sinatra ideal was for "truth, justice, and the American way." But Sinatra's cool was apart and above those old values. "Cool was looking out for number one always. Cool didn't get mad; it got even." Cool, as Kelly pointed out, is a cad. Cool isn't pious and certainly isn't virtuous. Cool is out for himself.

I have problems with that analysis, as Sinatra also spoke out against bigotry and lived his life opposed to racism at a time when that wasn't fashionable. He was a man helping to bring a new ideal, not simply a man all about himself, all about cool. Still, Kelly had a point. Sinatra was a post-Hemingway man, a post-Bogart man, a new breed of man creating a new definition, and he did leave manliness in a mixed-up age in which James Dean in *Rebel Without a Cause* asks what makes a man but is given no answers.

This is why I was on a quest to find the old values Hemingway was trying to refashion, in order to see if they might be brought to the new age of equality Sinatra was a part of. The man of this age might be enlightened, but he needs a foundation to put those new values on.

I knew that, by today's definition, the Hemingway man isn't cool. But he is an adventurer and a gentleman. He follows a code. He is a man having a hell of a time, not living a guilty life. He has Mark Twain's view of vices—and Sinatra's, for that matter. He thinks drinking, smoking, chewing tobacco, and using profanity are fine at the proper times and in the right proportions. He believes that vices can refine a man even though he is certain that vices shouldn't define a man. Still, to be closer to the modern ideal, he can't be a bigot, a sexist, or anything else that blocks the truth with the ignorant blinders of prejudgment.

But then, when I looked around at the people posing like characters in a painting at Les Deux Magots, I saw cool all over them. This made me feel sorry for women who date cool men. A cad isn't trustworthy. He is out for himself. He has no honor. He isn't a complete man. He is a boy in man's body.

This brings up an important misconception that must be put to rest right here. Some feminists attack "manliness" today for its past affronts on women and women's rights. Many also consider "Hemingway" to be a loaded term—stuffed with sexism, egotism, even misogyny. Some of that is true and all of that will be addressed as we go, but it should be pointed out right from the start that when we define "manliness" by character traits, not by fleeting physical attributes or loaded ideology, we must concede we're not only talking about men. I graduated from a military college with women as fellow cadets. I've run with the bulls in Pamplona alongside men and women. I've spelunked into caverns and climbed cliffs with men and women. Along the way, I've found that some of the most courageous and honorable people doing these things were women. I've also met and interviewed many fine police officers, US Marines, firefighters, and people in other occupations we consider to be manly and found that some of the best among them were also women. Obviously, what makes someone manly isn't about chromosomes, but about character.

Character, after all, must be the necessary measure of manliness, as physical definitions of manliness are shallow. To see what I mean, imagine an NFL linebacker panicking at the sight of blood and so failing to help an injured person in need. Would he be considered manly? In contrast, if a barely 100-pound, stooped-back man with arthritis shaking his knees did help the injured person, we would say he was manly, right?

From another angle, ask yourself if Mr. Olympia, 6-foot, 2-inch Arnold Schwarzenegger in *Conan the Barbarian*, is really manlier than slim, 5-foot, 7-inch Al Pacino in *The Godfather*.

Surely, physical traits can be signs of manliness. When we see a very out-of-shape person, we have reason to suspect they wouldn't be much help in a crisis. But, as we can't get in people's heads to read their character, we really can't know what their attributes and failings are. So again, we can only judge by their words and actions, not their physical appearance.

Despite this, a few still consider "manliness" to be akin to sexism, bravado, hubris. . . . To them I ask: Is a man who is so insecure that he has to prop up his own ego by putting down women really manly?

Obviously not.

Then is a woman who blindly attacks "manliness" as a threat really doing anyone any good? Surely such a person is guilty of a form of bigotry, even if it is fashionable in some circles. Though this is understandable given our history, isn't it time we grew beyond that blind judgment?

With this view of the character of real manliness in mind, I looked about that Paris café and saw that an intellectual who disdains his own masculinity is a fop, whereas a so-called masculine man who mocks the finer things is sentencing himself to Neolithic life. Many sense the absurdity of this chasm between the man of culture and the man of action, but few have come to any true answers to bring the two halves back together. The best example we have today is the now more-than-half-century-old 007, a character with the depth of a cartoon hero for sure, and the ethics of a cad; nevertheless, he is a man who can wear a tux and a diving suit with the same masculine strength, and he does fight for something other than himself.

No, manliness is not a simple concept, even though it is often treated as such. As I searched for these answers, I wasn't alone. I was with a group of men and women following the Hemingway trail from Paris to Pamplona all for our own reasons. We were going from the cafés, the art, the gardens of Paris to the brutality of running on Spanish streets with fighting bulls. The two places—Paris in summer and Pamplona during the San Fermín festival—appear so starkly different, it felt like we were transitioning from a Paul Cézanne post-impressionist landscape of plains of color building into green forests and softly lit yellow buildings to Francisco Goya's "black paintings," showing melting faces, devilish colors, and life frozen at the moment of rapture. Yet the Hemingway man, the iconic image he honed and presented in fiction, was at home in both Paris and Pamplona. By exhuming this Hemingway ideal, I hoped if not to resurrect a lost archetype, to at least understand what we've lost and maybe then to see how the two parts can be put back together again.

For bearings, before I left the US, I sought out the living authority on Hemingway, a college professor of literature and a poet who has lived in Paris and has been to Pamplona many times and, as this was being written, was the president of the Hemingway Society. I went to see Harry "Stoney" Stoneback at his home near New Paltz, New York.

His redbrick nineteenth-century home has brick walls around it and a lovely garden between old trees. The home is hidden in the forested edge of a small Hudson Valley town. Actually, his brick home could be frightening to a child in the wrong light, and the light I first saw it in was all wrong. Stoney was in the gazebo rosebushes had grown over. The late afternoon was dark. A summer thunderstorm had dimmed the sun, and lightening flashed to the west.

Stoney stood and walked with a badly stooped back as he led me inside the old brick home and closed a heavy oak door to the storm.

Once inside, he settled into a wheelchair and asked me to go into the dining room. He rolled his chair into his kitchen, and I soon heard glasses clinking and him rustling in a drawer for a corkscrew.

I took my time, as the home is a museum to an interesting man. There were books in French and English piled on tables and stacked along walls. Half-written poems were scribbled in the margins of open books and on yellow legal pads strewn on dark-wood end tables and chairs. Paintings purchased during sabbaticals to Paris, New Orleans, and China cluttered the walls. As I looked at them, I thought that a well-traveled man used to decorate his home with things that represent real things and places within his life. I thought that such a man wouldn't even comprehend a modern American suburbanite's habit of hanging pictures and displaying knickknacks because they match the color of the flat wall paint. An authentic man only hangs paintings and shelves books if they are pieces of an authentic life. Such an old-school man wouldn't have much to say to an urban sophisticate who displays Oriental or African art because it's hip; if the pieces aren't representative of who a person is, they shouldn't be on display, as without real meaning such things are only a façade hiding an inauthentic life, a fable there to impress visitors. So I was impressed that Stoney was all over the room and that he fit right into the scene, as it was an extension of him.

I sat down in the dining room at the end of a long cherry-varnished table that would seat ten if it wasn't so cluttered with books and scraps of paper slathered with half-written poems. The room felt like an ancient library half fallen in but came to life when Stoney rolled in, using his right hand to propel his wheelchair. He had a bottle of French red wine and two wineglasses in his left hand.

Stoney has a scraggly white beard and a crooked back broken from being pushed off an embankment by thieves in Cuba. This gives him a crumpled slouch when he walks. Photos on the walls, however, show he spent most of his life walking with shoulders wide enough and eyes high enough to stand even with Liam Neeson. One large photo is of Stoney and his now-departed wife. She has cake smeared on her face and is laughing in celebration of a birthday spent on a ship on the Hudson River. He told me this is his favorite picture, and he managed to keep tears out of his eyes as he said this, but not his voice.

I looked from the poster-sized photo to Stoney and saw that though he's now stooped into a wheelchair, his presence, charm, and intellect haven't diminished with his posture. His eyes are vivacious and his wit quick. He is still very much alive.

Stoney answered my polite questions simply but soon directed the conversation to what he knew I really wanted to know. He began by explaining he was a man of the times, of the 1960s and 1970s, when he began lecturing, but that through investigation he found the truth about Hemingway and himself and this truth shaped his life.

He told me in his professorial tone that he first discovered Ernest Hemingway when every boy should. When he was fifteen, he ran away from a Kentucky boarding school and hitchhiked east. Somewhere in West Virginia, he found himself at a truck stop drinking coffee and deciding where to go next when a waitress shushed the diner. She had a copy of *Life* magazine and wanted to read something to everyone. She began, "He was an old man who fished alone in a skiff . . ." She kept reading *The Old Man and the Sea*, and all the truck drivers sat listening, leaning back against the diner's chairs and over the counter. She read the entire story. When she finished over an hour later, the truck drivers banged their rough hands together and cheered.

Stoney looked around at the working-class men and women in the truck stop and conceded he had a lot to learn. There would be time enough for adventure along the way. He had to study. He hitched rides back to Kentucky and to school. Days later, in early September 1951, in a class on literature, his teacher said with this sniffing tone, "Everyone is now reading Hemingway's *The Old Man and the Sea*, but we're not going to read about the glorification of men who want to bring back a misogynous and patriarchal society. We're going to read Simone de Beauvoir's *The Second Sex*."

Stoney said he found this existential book on feminism important, but at the time he didn't realize what was happening to the view of manliness Hemingway articulated. He didn't then see what society was diminishing. Quite a long time later, he would push back against this feminist misunderstanding of Hemingway, but he had a lot to experience first.

Years later, he was in Paris as a young professor. While there, he says, "After work I could walk down the Boulevard Raspail to meet a friend at the Dôme and never once think of Hemingway. We would eat at Lipp's, go up on the hill afterwards, do the clubs, or go to a *bal-musette* where neighborhood locals still danced to an ancient accordion player, and never once think of Hemingway. . . . By the sheer force of cultural complicity, at least, I shared in the ill-informed condescension toward Hemingway that had become so fashionable in the 1960s."

At the time, he met the novelist James Jones in Paris, author of *The Merry Month of May*, and Jones looked him over and accused, "What are you, kid? Another young American novelist looking for Hemingway's ghost?"

Stoney said he was more interested in French writers like Baudelaire and Saint-John Perse, but Jones didn't believe him. Maybe Jones was out of touch with how Hemingway was seen as passé by American university professors, or even that Hemingway was disdained by many as an aged icon of a false and sexist epoch. Maybe Jones just didn't know how a product of this system might be disposed.

Whatever Jones knew and thought, Stoney shrugged and forgot all about the accusation. He went to poetry readings at the Paris bookstore Shakespeare & Company—a bookstore Hemingway often borrowed books from. In the 1920s, Paris's Shakespeare & Company was owned by Sylvia Beach and was then located at 12 Rue de l'Odéon. Hemingway was then young and poor. Beach gave him a card for her lending library and told him to pay when he could. Hemingway used the card voraciously to educate himself.

Now the iconic bookstore is located on the quay across from Notre Dame. While there for poetry readings in the early 1970s, Stoney listened as an American youth with a monotone and feckless voice attacked Hemingway's "phony machismo" and "woman hating," but again Stoney didn't ponder this for very long. He didn't then know finding the truth about these claims would soon fill the bulk of his intellectual life.

Stoney's eyes opened to another Paris, to Hemingway's Paris, in 1974 when he happened upon a copy of *The Sun Also Rises* at Shakespeare & Company. Stoney was then in Paris as a visiting professor teaching a course on Faulkner at the University of Paris. He hadn't read the novel in years and bought a copy to reacquaint himself. He says, "I read the novel in my Paris apartment. As I read, I looked out my window across the Rue Saint-Jacques to Val-de-Grace, and Hemingway's Paris came alive for me."

He realized Hemingway had embedded the *deus loci*, the spirit of place, of Paris in him long before. He asked himself: "How can a casual reading of a novel years before implant the spirit of a place in me?" For answers, he began walking the places Hemingway described as he explored the places Jake, the main character in *The Sun Also Rises*, did and found one puzzling incongruity, an oddity that would turn out to be a key to understanding the Hemingway man our society has misunderstood and all but slain.

He was puzzled by Hemingway's description of the Rue Saint-Jacques, a street in the Latin Quarter of Paris that was a main axial road of medieval Paris. Hemingway described it as "the rigid north and south of the Rue Saint-Jacques." But this street isn't "rigid"; actually, it's a medieval street that bends. Why would such a master of detail get a street he knew well wrong? Stoney asked a Parisian friend who was a lover of history. His friend replied by asking, "Do you know of Saint-Jacques de Compostelle?" Stoney said he didn't. His friend asked, "Do you know, then, Santiago de Compostela?" Stoney said he did. Santiago de Compostela is a church in Spain that is at the end of ancient Christian pilgrim routes known as the El Camino de Santiago ("Way of Saint James"). The ancient paths lead from France to the shrine of the apostle St. James the Great in the Cathedral of Santiago de Compostela in Galicia.

"More than a place, my friend. Come, walk with me," said Stoney's friend.

They walked along the Rue Saint-Jacques. His friend pointed out that Val-de-Grace was a well-known church, monastery, and a hospital used for the wounded in World War I. The additions, added to the street in the nineteenth century, are what seem rigid. Stoney could see this and said so, but there was more, much more. His friend explained that the place's inclusion in the novel has a deep importance. This site was a religious step on the Way to St. James. There was even a hospice there for those traveling the holy path. The hospital for wounded soldiers was also important because Jake had a war wound that made him impotent. Stoney found that Hemingway had Jake symbolically following the path to heal his spirit, a journey to Spain he took every year. This was a journey Hemingway took many times while he lived in Paris. As someone who'd been wounded in World War I, Hemingway knew of these things and was affected by them. He used them in his writing as devices to give the novel its unseen depths that people sense but so often don't completely comprehend.

Stoney was intrigued and started to dig. He found that even the name "Jake" marked Hemingway's main character in *The Sun Also Rises* as a pilgrim, as the *Liber Sancti Jacobi* (also known as the "Codex Calixtinus") is a twelfth-century anthology of background detail and advice for pilgrims following the Way of St. James. Also, in the Old Testament, Jacob wrestled with the angel all night. They wrestled to a draw, and the angel (described only as a "man") touches Jacob in the "socket of his thigh," hobbling him. The angel then tells him, "Your name shall no longer be Jacob, but Israel; for you have striven with God and with men and have prevailed." Jacob then forever after had "the power with God and with men." His life was then "preserved," and "the sun rose upon him."[3] Stoney found that Hemingway had given the character the name Jake with this biblical reference in mind. He discovered that Hemingway sent Jake on a holy pilgrimage to heal, not his wounded body, but his soul, and to help his companions do the same.

I've found this isn't another theory from a professor reading between the lines to sound smarter than the rest of us. Stoney, for example, found that while writing *The Sun Also Rises*, Hemingway visited the philosopher Ralph Church. Church had just published *The Essence of Catholicism* (1924). Stoney notes that in Church's unpublished memoirs, he says Hemingway referred to his upcoming novel as a "pilgrimage to Pamplona." Church wrote that "Hemingway was deeply interested in the problem of redemption."

Letters to his friends at this time also show his interest in Christianity. On July 19, 1924, while he was in Pamplona for the San Fermín fiesta, Hemingway wrote Ezra Pound to tell him "I prayed to St. Fermin for you. Not that you needed it but I found myself in Mass with nothing to do and so prayed for my kid, for Hadley, for myself and your concert."

A few years later, on January 2, 1926, Hemingway wrote to Ernest Walsh and told him: "If I am anything I am a Catholic. Had extreme unction administered to me as such in July, 1918 and recovered. So guess I am a super-catholic.

---

[3]Genesis 32:24-31.

. . . Am not what is called a 'good' catholic. . . . But cannot imagine taking any other religion seriously."

Though his novel was first titled *Lost Generation* and then *Fiesta*, Hemingway finally crafted the title *The Sun Also Rises* from biblical verses in Ecclesiastes: "One generation passeth away, and another generation cometh; but the earth abideth forever. The sun also ariseth, and the sun goeth down, and hasteth to the place where he arose." He wanted to point the Lost Generation toward optimism—the sun doesn't just set with war, it also rises afterward.

As the novel progresses, Hemingway shows us through Jake, often by contrast to the character Robert Cohn, the codified behavior he lives by—the rules grounding and defining the Hemingway man. Stoney found that understanding Jake was on a pilgrimage, and was acting as a guide to a group of wayward people caught in the meaningless drinking and promiscuity of the Lost Generation, is a key that opens a door to the unwritten code Hemingway was obsessed with.

This code is often overlooked partly because of what Hemingway called his "theory of omission." Hemingway once wrote: "If a writer of prose knows enough about what he is writing about he may omit things that he knows and the reader, if the writer is writing truly enough, will have a feeling of those things as strongly as though the writer had stated them. The dignity of movement of an ice-berg is due to only one-eighth of it being above water."[4] Hemingway felt this theory of omission applied to fine writing. He thought

---

[4]Ernest Hemingway, *Death in the Afternoon*, Scribner's, New York, 1932.

that what is known, but only implied, can be more important than what is said by an author. Stoney said, with Hemingway, the tips of the icebergs "are the spires and towers of the cathedrals and churches which compose the skylines of his narratives."

As he discovered all this, Stoney knew he was going against the intellectual grain of what was then in vogue in academia, so in 1974 he asked Allen Tate (1899–1979), a poet and critic who had been friends with Hemingway in Paris in 1929, about Hemingway. Tate said Hemingway was "very Catholic." He said he had gone to Mass with Hemingway. He said that though Hemingway thought he wasn't always a good Catholic, he was nevertheless rooted in its moral tradition. Accounts like this told Stoney he was on the right path.

During his search for answers in the wilderness of academia, Stoney said he had other literary evenings in Paris with French and American writers "in lavish penthouses off Etoile and private receptions for artists" and that he found that "in spite of their condescension to Hemingway as some kind of outré fisherman or gauche big-game hunter, bully, self-parodic monosyllabic mutterer, many were really trying to relive Hemingway's Paris, trying too hard and doing it with infinitely less style, grace, intelligence, and discipline." He said he wasn't at first sure what Hemingway's overlooked and unfashionable Catholicism had to do with the code Hemingway was articulating through Jake in *The Sun Also Rises* and in so much of his other work, but that by degrees he began to see it as the key to understanding Hemingway—and to understanding why so many have been drawn to Hemingway ever since.

With this insight in mind, I left Les Deux Magots with the group of American Hemingway aficionados. We were a group of four men and three women that would wax and wane as friends joined us and parted in Paris and along the Hemingway trail. At forty, I was the youngest in the group. Most of them were members of the Hemingway Society and had followed the Hemingway trail from Paris to Pamplona many times.

We stepped around three people playing jazz softly on the sidewalk and lingered with dozens of others. We talked about the harmony of the scene, and someone noted that Hemingway, even as he loved Paris, didn't embrace all these people. Hemingway had contempt for café trash. He called them the "weird lot" in a 1922 article titled "American Bohemians in Paris." He wrote: "The scum of Greenwich Village, New York, has been skimmed off and deposited in large ladlesful on the section of Paris adjacent to the Café Rotunde. New scum, of course, has risen to take the place of the old, but the oldest scum, the thickest scum, and the scummiest scum has come across the ocean, somehow, and with its afternoon and evening levees has made the Rotunde the leading Latin quarter show place for tourists in search of atmosphere. It is a strange-acting and strange-looking breed that crowd the tables of the Café Rotunde. They have all striven so hard for careless individuality of clothing that they have achieved a sort of uniformity of eccentricity."

Hemingway was a conservative even in his age, but seeing all this made it clear that his modern stereotype is empty, even dishonest. Sure, he liked guns and hunting and fishing, but he was far too well educated and traveled to be called a redneck.

He read prodigiously and wrote elegant prose and loved a refined drink and collected fine art, but he also enjoyed a cowboy brawl. He divorced many times and was likely an alcoholic a good portion of his life, but he was a romantic who married and converted to Catholicism to improve himself. He went mad at the end and killed himself, but he lived life on the seas and in foreign countries and on battlefields and went on safaris and always seemed to be having a hell of a time. To deflate his persona from all this and much more to something that could be easily flushed, his detractors had to simplify and parody him until his real story faded into a fragment of the truth.

Still, even the most gifted critic can't talk away what's real. Hemingway was complex, secretive, and deliberately fashioned his public persona. His critics aren't the central reason he is often misunderstood today; he kicked up mystery around himself to fashion a certain tough-guy, man-of-the-world persona, and many are confused by that aura.

As for the "café trash," the truth is that even as he mocked them, he also mingled with them and was drawn to those among them who weren't imposters, to those who were really trying to be painters, writers, and other things. His friend and later biographer, A. E. Hotchner, noted that Hemingway preferred people who were boldly being what they seemed.

A flamboyant example of this love of people who are living honestly can be found in Hemingway's *Death in the Afternoon* (1932). He asks: "You went to the bullfight? How was it?" One person answers "disgusting," and Hemingway gives him an "honorable discharge." Another says "terrible" and gets the same pass. Then one says, "I was simply bored to death." Hemingway says, "All right. You get the hell out of here." If your eyes are open and you're honest, you're fine, but if you are sleepwalking through life or hiding behind a false front, you better get the hell away. Certainly such a view could rub some people—the critics, the fake artists, the posers—the wrong way.

Hemingway, of course, wasn't all show. He worked. As he did, he defended his privacy from those living false lives. When Hemingway lived in Paris, he sought out quiet cafés, such as those on the Place Saint-Michel, to write in, and he noted in the posthumously published *A Moveable Feast* how he loathed those who bothered him when he was working in a café. To Hemingway, there was a code of conduct to how one behaved, even in the cafés. Not understanding the code was no excuse. Such a person must be taught to behave.

He became friends with Picasso and F. Scott Fitzgerald and many other painters and writers, and at times relied on their generosity to pay his rent. What he saw in the "café trash" were rich brats with loose morals and tragic lives who couldn't be trusted with a dime, because they weren't really suffering to become the artists they claimed to be; whereas those who were in Paris to become something real, those people who slaved at their passion and trade learned about real honor through toil and failure and so could more often be trusted and respected.

After writing in a quiet café or in one of his apartments, Hemingway would go to the Le Dôme Café or Café de la Rotonde. He'd revel in the conversation and the drinks, always he was very detailed about the drinks and how a man enjoys them but also handles them. He actually preferred the

Closerie des Lilas to the Dôme and Rotonde, as he thought the Closerie less ostentatious. He wrote that the "Closerie des Lilas was the nearest good café when we lived in the flat over the sawmill at 113 Rue Notre-Dame-des-Champs, and it was one of the best cafés in Paris."[5] He said it was a place where no one was on "exhibition." Still, he went to all of the fashionable cafés. Hemingway tells us, "In those days many people went to the cafés at the corner of the Boulevard Montparnasse and the Boulevard Raspail to be seen publicly and in a way such places anticipated the columnists as the daily substitutes for immortality."

So we went to Café de la Rotonde at the corner of Boulevard du Montparnasse and Boulevard Raspail. This was a place Picasso painted and where the painter Diego Rivera frequented, and also that Tsuguharu Foujita drew. We found the walls and ceilings were bright with gaudy colors twisting in rainbows of shapes from what trend in art none us could name. We ordered martinis and had to explain how to make them in our poor French, and we smiled at the helpful but bemused conduct of the waiter. The café was crowded in the evening and well-lighted by chandeliers and was full of decorative people.

The next day we had coffee and brioche in the Luxembourg Gardens where Hemingway said (maybe joked) he used to trap pigeons for dinner. We talked about how Hemingway thought of hunger as a "good discipline" and wrote "you could always go into the Luxembourg Museum and all the paintings were sharper and clearer and more beautiful if you

---

[5]Ernest Hemingway, *A Moveable Feast*, Scribner's, New York, 1964.

were belly-empty, hollow-hungry. I learned to understand Cézanne much better and to see truly how he made landscapes when I was hungry." When the hunger finally became too much, Hemingway said he'd go to Brasserie Lipp, which is still there, where he might enjoy a cold liter of beer with *pommes à l'huile* and sausage.

We followed his steps to Lipp's and to many other places and later paused to laugh outside what was once Michaud's, a place Hemingway says was "on the corner of the rue Jacob and the rue des Saints-Pères." This is where Hemingway says F. Scott Fitzgerald asked him to look at his manhood. Fitzgerald's wife Zelda said the way he "was built . . . could never make any woman happy." Hemingway went into the bathroom with Fitzgerald, took a look, and said, "You are O.K." When Fitzgerald still wasn't certain, Hemingway said he took him to the Louvre to look at "the people in the statues." Fitzgerald worried that the "statues might not be accurate," but Hemingway assured him that "most people would settle for them."

Fitzgerald asked if he was okay, then why would Zelda say he wasn't and Hemingway replied, "To put you out of business. That's the oldest way in the world of putting people out of business."[6]

Fitzgerald still wasn't sure and Hemingway gave up. To Hemingway, it is manly to patiently instruct, but you couldn't give another person courage. Men need to earn courage on their own, which is what rites of passage are all about.

Hemingway later blamed Fitzgerald's weakness for and his inability to handle alcohol and fame for his downfall.

---

[6]Ernest Hemingway, *A Moveable Feast*, Scribner's, 1964.

He also placed some blame on Zelda for destroying, out of jealousy, the talent Fitzgerald clearly had.

We next saw the places Hemingway lived in and the impressionist painters and others he said shaped his prose, and we went to other cafés that still exist where Hemingway, James Joyce, Dos Passos, and the rest of that literary crowd drank and even worked. Looking at Paris this way, and at the art he studied, it became clear how Paris influenced his simple but beautiful style of writing he called a "severe discipline," as the lines of the city are clean, simple, and beautiful and even the gaudier things—the Louvre, the bridges, and cathedrals—are sparkling jewels around the neck of an elegantly dressed woman.

Still, as we went to these places and left them one by one, it became clear we also must leave Ernest Hemingway the real man for a while to see what he was showing us. Many writers have critically investigated Hemingway's attributes and his failings. There are guides written for people who want to drink where he did (we were following *Walks in Hemingway's Paris* and others). Still more have tried to step out of Hemingway's shadow by capturing the *deus loci* of Paris in prose. What I'm after here is something that has been missed or lost. I'm trying to understand the tangible meaning behind the iconic image Hemingway put on paper, a persona that was alluring, even if misunderstood, even in his age, a manly character many are still drawn to today even if they can't quite express what they find so captivating.

For these deeper answers, it's helpful to turn to Hemingway's two central characters in *The Sun Also Rises*, to Jake Barnes and Robert Cohn. By contrast, they define the

Hemingway man. All we need is Stoney's key to know this well-rounded man.

Jake is the narrator and central character of *The Sun Also Rises*. He is a foreign correspondent working in Paris who brings all the novel's characters together for a journey from Paris to Pamplona. Robert, in contrast, is a thirty-four-year-old novelist spoiled by his own success. He's lost and self-centered. Robert has been called a representative of what was then deemed the "Lost Generation," a label Gertrude Stein invented and that Hemingway mocked.

Jake fought in World War I and was left impotent from a war wound. He was in love with Lady Brett—the main female character in the novel—but he couldn't consummate his love. She loved him, too, and that is their tragedy. Sometime before the action in the novel begins, they seem to have come to an understanding about this and have decided to make a go at being friends. To overcome this suffering, Jake, we find as he goes on, steadied himself by standing firm upon values he sees as real and by trying to help the others do the same. Unlike so many men today, he never talks about his sad dilemma. He just lives with it while trying not to let it define him.

That is the plot people know. It's what goes on through and beneath the action in the novel that is both missed and loved for what it portends.

Late in the editing process—at the urging of Fitzgerald—Hemingway cut his opening chapters from *The Sun Also Rises*. Perhaps he found them too obvious, but if people had read these, Jake's Catholicism would have been clearer. In the deleted section, Jake says, "So my name is Jacob Barnes and

I am writing the story, not as I believe is usual in these cases, from a desire for confession, because being a Roman Catholic I am spared that Protestant urge to literary production."

With the front lopped off, the novel as we know it begins with Robert Cohn. Hemingway tells us in the first sentences that Robert was once the "middleweight boxing champion of Princeton. Do not think that I am very much impressed by that as a boxing title, but it meant a lot to Cohn." Right away, Hemingway tells us Robert is uncomfortable with himself. Before long, another character (Harvey) gives us a more critical opinion of Robert. Harvey says to Robert, "I misjudged you. You're not a moron. You're only a case of arrested development." Robert is the immature man.

Robert could be the insecure urban man of today's age. He's unproven and senses this about himself. He behaves as a boy and dislikes himself for this, but he can see no better way. He's self-centered and childish and confuses masculinity with school yard–style fights—which is why the first thing we find is he has a meaningless boxing title.

Robert Cohn is like F. Scott Fitzgerald's character Tom Buchanan in *The Great Gatsby*, a novel Hemingway read closely before beginning *The Sun Also Rises*. Buchanan was a former football player at Yale who, as Fitzgerald writes, "reached such an acute limited excellence at twenty-one that everything afterward savors of anticlimax."

Robert is also like Hemingway's character Francis in the short story *The Short Happy Life of Francis Macomber*. Hemingway says Francis Macomber was "thirty-five years old [Robert was thirty-four], kept himself very fit, was good at court games . . . and had just shown himself, very publicly, to be a coward." Francis drops his gun and runs from a charging lion he'd wounded. His professional hunter, Robert Wilson (played by Gregory Peck in the movie), stands his ground and kills the lion. When they return to camp, Wilson has the quiet confidence of a man who has proven himself and the humility of a man who is so secure he doesn't need to say so.

Francis's manliness, meanwhile, has a yellow hole shot right through it. Wilson knows this but is reluctant to talk about it. Saying such things aloud, he believes, only intensifies the trouble. Best to leave such failings to the quiet parts of a man's mind, where he can turn them over and learn from them without being publicly scarred by them. Men only talk about such things privately with a pal or a professional at rare times when they're under great stress. Immediately after the talk is supposed to be forgotten; it's a mere human digression best left to the darkening shadows of the past—something to be learned from, not something that should negatively define a man's character. This is the old-school view of such things.

Hemingway practiced this belief. He told his friend A. E. Hotchner he went to "doctors" when he'd become impotent after parting from his first wife, Hadley. Hemingway had been having an affair in Paris with Pauline Pfeiffer, who became his second wife. He said, after Hadley was gone, "suddenly I could no more make love than Jake Barnes." After the tries with psychologists, Pauline said to him: "Listen, Ernest, why don't you go and pray." Pauline was Catholic. Hemingway went to a small Catholic chapel and prayed and said he then went home and "we made love like we invented it. We never had any trouble again. That's when I became a

Catholic." Like a lot of Hemingway's tales of triumph, it's hard to say how much truth is in this story. What it certainly tells us, though, is he thought manliness requires a great deal of stoicism and discretion sprinkled with the strong, ego-saving spice of bravado. Hemingway only mentioned sex when it was some kind of conquest, either over a woman or over himself.

So when Francis wants to talk about the cowardice he exhibited when the lion charged, Wilson tells him it is done and should be left in the field. Wilson implies that Francis will have other chances to redeem himself as long as he doesn't stop trying, as long as he doesn't let it grow into a defining characteristic. Francis pushes for comforting words until he begins to whine. Wilson does all he can to let it drop. He thinks Francis should keep a stiff upper lip and bear trouble like a man and all that grandfatherly advice. Francis doesn't grasp this. He keeps pushing Wilson as a child would.

Still, though Wilson's code of conduct dictates the definition of manliness in the short story, like Hemingway, Wilson was hardly a saint. When Francis's wife—who deplores her husband's stench of cowardice—comes to Wilson's tent that night, Wilson sleeps with her. Wilson isn't a Sir Galahad or any other Christian hero. He's a real man with lust and failings. Wilson even goes on safari with a double-wide cot just in case one of the wives wants a go at the "white hunter." Wilson has decided, Hemingway tells us, that on safari his clients' ethics are his. His clients are rich and spoiled, so their ethics are as loose and as childish as Fitzgerald's Tom Buchanan or Hemingway's Robert Cohn.

Wilson, meanwhile, thinks, but keeps it to himself, that he doesn't understand how American men "stay little boys so long. . . . Sometimes all their lives. . . . The great American boy-men."

Later, of course, Francis would redeem his manhood by standing up to a charging Cape buffalo in a real rite of passage, but Robert never would, and that is all the difference.

Actually, from the first to the last pages, Robert is a great American boy-man. While still in Paris, Robert bothers Jake at work. Jake makes it clear he's on deadline but says he can talk for a little while. Robert selfishly ignores Jake's need to get his article done by press time. Robert is at a crossroads in his life and wants to run away to a fantasy. To accomplish this, he asks Jake to come to South America with him. He'd just read W. H. Hudson's book *The Purple Land* and came away with very romantic ideas of how his life might be better in such a faraway hinterland of jungles and primitive peoples. Jake, in contrast, shows no interest in pursuing Robert's ever-moving fantasyland and tells him so. Jake is grounding himself in real experiences; Robert is desperately trying to stay in a child's fantasyland.

As the action in the novel develops, it is Jake's grounded and well-ordered life that gives the novel its cohesive adventure, but Jake doesn't paint his transformative path into a purple land of dreamscapes. Jake is doing all he can to live in reality and with his real condition.

To help Robert, Jake tells him to start living his life in Paris, as Paris is a good town. Robert replies that he doesn't like Paris. He only came to Paris because it was fashionable.

He then complains he has the sense he's not really living life "all the way up." Jake explains that what he's looking for isn't in South America, as he'd still be himself in South America. He has to start looking under his feet.

Robert doesn't understand, so Jake uses the bullfighter as a metaphor to explain that a man needs to live here and now with grace, honor, and courage, because death is charging us all the time. Robert either isn't listening or doesn't understand the codified behavior Jake is grounded on. Robert just says bullfighters live "an abnormal life."

Stoney believes this is the central question in the novel. "Given our mortality," said Stoney, "the evanescent transience of life, how do we live our lives authentically and passionately every day of the short time we have? One answer, for Jake, is epitomized and symbolized by the bullfighter, who looks death in the face in the arena, who confronts mortality—if he does his job well—with dignity, poise, passion, discipline, and highly formalized grace under pressure, and achieves a ritual and communal sense of immortality."

Order just isn't something Robert grasps. He's looking inward and so can't see the ground under his feet. Still, Jake tries. Jake suggests hunting in Africa instead—hunting is another real life-death ritual that has actual and bloody consequences. Jake seems to think that if Robert were to take a hunt seriously it could ground him by helping him prove himself.

Robert, however, doesn't embrace these real experiences. He wants the fantasy he read about. He almost turns red and stomps his feet when Jake won't give it to him. Jake finally gets impatient and tells Robert to go and read some books on Africa. Maybe then he'll get romantic notions about the Dark Continent. Robert, though, only wants his way. So Jake tries to get Robert out of his office by taking him out for a drink and, after the drink, telling him he has to get back to work. Robert doesn't take the polite hint. He just follows Jake back to his office. Stoney summed this up by saying, "Codified behavior doesn't work with Robert because he doesn't get the code."[7]

Not nearly. Early in the novel, Robert's fiancé Frances even emasculates Robert in front of Jake. After a long engagement—waiting for her divorce—Robert can't bring himself to commit to the mature oath of marriage. Nor can he break it off like a mature man should. So, right in front of Robert, Frances complains to Jake that Robert is "so childish" that he "cries and begs me to be reasonable." She even advises Robert on his writing by telling him: "Don't have scenes with your young ladies. Try not to. Because you can't have scenes without crying, and then you pity yourself so much you can't remember what the other person said."

Soon, instead of South America, Jake invites Robert and others along on his annual trip to Spain. He wants to show his friends his pilgrimage, but he is reluctant to explain any of this to them. They have to see, to feel for themselves.

So they follow the path from Paris toward Santiago de Compostela, as millions of pilgrims over more than a thousand years have. And so do we. After drinking in Hemingway's

---

[7]H. R. Stoneback, *Reading The Sun Also Rises*, The Kent State University Press, Kent, Ohio, 2007.

famed cafés, and seeing the art, the light on the storied bou-
levards and buildings, the ornate bridges along the Seine, the
iconic architecture, the style of life that inspired and refined
Hemingway into the writer he became, we boarded a train
at Montparnasse Station and followed the path to Pamplona
and the pass of Roland, as all of these were steps in Hemingway's and Jake's pilgrimages on the Way to Saint James.

We'd tasted the sophisticated side of the Hemingway
man but needed to experience the wilder side to understand
the depth and action of his character. This is what anyone
entering a real rite of passage must do. If someone wants to
be a nurse, a baseball player, or a businessman, they need to
understand who they're trying to become.

Americans today are often taught to try different things as
they search for a calling. When you find something that pleases
you, you're supposed to simply follow that path. You're not
asked to understand your vision, just to follow its Yellow Brick
Road. This is an almost impossible thing to accomplish in a
world of visual distractions. Many become lost on such dark
and uneven roads to manhood. Joseph Campbell once said this
is why so many people today "climb a ladder and sometime in
their thirties find the ladder is against the wrong wall."[8]

If instead you first try to see, then to understand, who
you want to be, you'll catch glimpses of your ideal moving
tauntingly away. He is not you, but he might be. He is whom
you wish to be, whom you wish to be seen as. He is an idea
that can transport you up into the next level of your life, but
he is fleeting. We must pursue with our minds and bodies.

---

[8]Joseph Campbell, *The Hero's Journey,* HarperCollins, New York, 1990.

We must follow an ideal in an age that doesn't trust ideals. When we do, he'll lead us into a rite of passage.

To really understand the Hemingway man in this rite of passage, I next had to shoulder my way onto a crowded Spanish street and run with fighting bulls.

STEP 2

The Terror and the Confusion

Cowardice, as distinguished from panic, is almost always simply a lack of ability to suspend the functioning of the imagination.

—Ernest Hemingway, an introduction to *Men at War*

EACH OF US STOOD ALONE in an anxious crowd. There were so many of us filling the narrow street in Pamplona that I had to turn my shoulders and push against the crowd to move. We were all wearing white clothes with red sashes and bandanas bought from street vendors in the small city. The veteran runners' sashes and bandanas were washed-out red and they had patches sewn on them and shiny pins of bulls and runners clustered over them like Boy

Scout bandanas. Most of the people in the street had new and clean red bandanas and sashes.

Morning sunlight was touching the tops of five-story stone buildings that rise up like walls along the narrow streets in this ancient city built on a plateau in the Pyrenees. At each floor above the first are balconies. These were overloaded with people also dressed in white and red, though the people on them had blood and wine, not fear, in their eyes. The clear mountain air just before 8:00 a.m. felt as humid as New Orleans in summer within the nervous crowd of runners.

Outside the packed street, music was building and falling as marching bands moved down the canyon streets closer, then away, twisting with the curving byways back into the city founded by Romans.

The bulls run every morning at 8:00 a.m. for eight days in a row. You have to get in the street before 7:30 a.m., as that's when the police close the entrances through the wooden barricades to the narrow streets where the bulls run. You move to find a good position. You hope you've chosen well. You think about when you'll begin to run. Mostly you stand and wait. Thirty minutes is a long time to ponder riding the horns. It had almost been thirty minutes already.

I couldn't see how the bulls could make it up the street. I've had less trouble squeezing onto Tokyo subways than this tiny street in Spain. I stood feeling as if I were in a mosh pit at a heavy metal concert—a concert where someone was about to release bulls.

Each minute, loudspeakers hung up and down the street were doing a countdown to the planned stampede. They were giving advice in Spanish, English, and French: "If you are knocked down. Stay down. Don't stand up in front of a bull. . . ."

As I stood shoulder-to-shoulder with men and a few women in white shirts and pants and red sashes and bandanas, everyone looked up and jeered as a young man and woman climbed a drainpipe. The couple shinnied up the pipe to an empty balcony two floors up. The man went first over the black iron rail and then turned to help the woman. She struggled and almost fell. He caught her arm and dragged her up too forcefully. Her dress caught on the balcony's rail, and everyone in the street got a long look at her bright blue panties. She was caught there with her legs spread and toes pointing at the sky and her dress falling over his chest. The man with his arms grabbing her wrists was almost flat on his back on the balcony. The crowd of mostly young men below began to cheer. She finally tumbled onto the balcony and everyone laughed like it was the funniest thing they'd ever seen.

The light moment flitted away. Stomach acid seeped into my mouth. I again wondered how the bulls could get through the packed street. I looked up at blue sky and saw the onlookers overcrowding tiny steel balconies for five stories above, all longing to witness the mayhem to come. Below them were people, perched legs dangling atop the outside wooden barricades all along the jostling street. They'd been there so long, their urine wet the pavement below them. There were two sets of barriers. In between the wooden barricades were police officers. The officers were all tall dark men in blue tight uniforms and expressions passing from stoic to bemusement.

I was where the festival began two days before with the *chupinazo*, a celebration that explodes when the mayor shoots a rocket at noon. When the rocket goes off, people pour water and wine from the balconies on a dancing, singing horde. Since the opening ceremony, the wine had mixed with urine, vomit, and other things. I shuffled my feet on cobblestones and hoped I wouldn't slip on the grimy stone and fall sprawling under the bulls.

I didn't see Juan Macho, my guide to surviving the *encierro* (the running of the bulls). I was being pushed one way then back again by people from perhaps every country in Europe and other parts of the world, yet I felt more alone than ever before. Soon people began diving from the balconies onto the street that really was a mosh pit for the fleeting minute.

A group of Brits from some football team began singing and locking arms as they bounced on the balls of their feet, finding courage in one another. They knocked into me and everyone else and from above must have looked like a muscle spasm in a long and shuddering snake of people filling the tight streets. Somewhere a peña played. Its drums echoed like a far-off avalanche rumbling to the bottom of a Rocky Mountain canyon.

That recurring announcement broadcast in many languages kept blaring like a conscience: "If you're knocked down, stay down until the bulls pass. . . ."

Minutes before 8:00 a.m., medical workers hurried into spots alongside policemen positioned between the double set of barriers on both sides of the street. Runners next to me saw the medical teams and caved in upon their manhood. *This is real. It is happening. There is no escape.*

The crowd began to shudder in waves like flinches.

One such tremor broke an American next to me. Minutes before, we'd been shouting introductions to each other, and he'd been relatively in control of himself. Since then, he'd become delirious with fear. He shouted some awful thing and tried to crawl under the heavy wooden fence and away.

A Spanish cop kicked him in the head, sending him back out alongside me. Blood dribbled from a small cut on his forehead.

Many other runners were losing their nerve. Some were running early. The Spanish call those who run before the bulls arrive *"valientes,"* which ironically translates to "brave ones." With their departure there was suddenly elbow room. I anxiously stretched. I looked back to where the bulls would come and breathed deep. I glanced left and saw that the American who'd tried to go under the fence looked like someone right out of one of Goya's *Los Desastres de la Guerra* (The Disasters of War) paintings.

His eyes were too big. His mouth was roving around his suddenly fluid face. He had gone mad. He had to get out. He dropped onto the ground and rolled under the fence.

The cop waiting on the other side clubbed him with his three-foot-long baton and kicked him back into the street. Then the officer bellowed something in the heart-pounding scene I'll never forget: "You wanted to be a man and run with the bulls; now you must be a man and run with the bulls."

The Spanish officer's face was granite. He had the stiff, proud bearing of a drill sergeant. He wasn't to be trifled with. But the American didn't want to die. Half the runners had already fled toward the arena. Those still waiting were set like sprinters—though with out-of-control expressions of people who see a car skidding off the road right for them.

"*Nooo!*"

The American went under the fence a third time. The cop swung his club with calculated viciousness, but the American was too panicked to notice. The officer picked up the American who wouldn't be a man and tossed him into a brick wall behind the fence. The American fell limp, wetting himself as he slid to the stone street. The cop batted the club in his left palm and looked at the street full of runners as if to ask, "Anyone else?"

Eight a.m. exploded with a *Boom!* A rocket announced that the bull pen had been thrown open. No one in the street heard the second rocket telling us all the bulls were out and running up the hill in the first part of the course. We had seconds. A moving roar echoed closer. Spectators on the balconies saw the bulls first. Six black Spanish fighting bulls and six steers running to guide them to the bullfighting arena were almost on us.

The bulls were stampeding. There is no other word for how the six black fighting bulls and the steers leading them run the uphill portion and then the first two turns of the course. People's faces were melting as the roar went up from the people in white and red overloading the balconies on the yellow buildings with the upper floors bathed in early sun.

I ran while glancing over my right shoulder at the mad faces behind me and back again to the parting sea of runners ahead. Someone went down in front of me in a white screaming blur. I leapt over him. Someone knocked me right, near the outside of a bend in the street just beyond the mayor's mansion. I knew that spot is death, as the bulls run the street like a current—most of the water hits the far bank in a bend, and this happens to bulls running on slick stone even more than it does a stream's current.

I pushed back left. Wild eyes and screams were telling me the bulls were close. I didn't need them to tell me this. The bulls' hooves were pounding, slamming into the hard street right behind me. They were deafening.

I spotted a hole and dodged left between white blurs of people and then the black bulls with the forward-facing horns were by me and pounding away toward the arena where they would die that afternoon.

After the bulls run the course, "sweepers" (a group of steers) are sent down the course to pick up any *suelto* (lone) bulls that might have become separated on the run. The bulls have a herding instinct and so will join the steers— animals that have run the course many times—and thereby push on to the pens on the opposite side of the bullfighting arena. This is important, as a lone bull is dangerous. The gorings that make newscasts are mostly from *suelto* bulls that have fallen or were turned around and so found themselves alone. When they're alone, they see all the people as a threat that must be destroyed. They'll often pick one person and start goring them until experienced runners get the bull's attention and persuade him to follow them down the street.

Now, some of the guidebooks tell you to count the fighting bulls when they pass you on the street so you can be certain the six fighting bulls are gone and there isn't a *suelto* making its way through the crowd toward you. I always wonder if the authors of these guidebooks ever ran and so tried to count running bulls in a crowded street as your heart is in your churning feet.

This time the bulls had all passed, and, as always happens in this moment of relief and joy, the street began to smile. People were checking themselves. A few were limping. The air was cool and mountain clear again. Medical workers were helping a man with a bloody leg. A young man from Canada had blood on his face. He was laughing. I ask what happened. He said excitedly, "Oh, someone pushed me over from behind, and I went sliding along on my face."

There was black bull hair on the back of his white shirt. I pointed this out to him and he pulled a few off and got this saucer-eyed expression and really started to laugh so hard he had to bend over and put his hands on his knees.

I put my right hand on his shoulder and while laughing with him told him I'm buying the drinks. We were instantly friends. We went through the barriers and up a side street that was still wet from being hosed clean yet still smelling like a wet basement after a teenage all-night kegger. There were empty beer bottles and plastic cups in the gutters. There were a few blurry-eyed people sitting drunk in the detritus.

We stepped into Pamplona's central square, wide as two football fields and as long as four. The sun was hot already, and people everywhere were streaming in, smiling life with their white clothes sweaty and smudged and their red sashes swinging as they walked.

Bars with wide flapping awnings run around the Plaza del Castillo. Many of the tables were already crowded. Some were filled with Basques, but many were foreigners. Two legends attempt to explain the red-and-white uniform almost everyone wears all during this festival: one says it's to honor the

Catholic saint San Fermín, white for the saint and red show-ing he was a martyr; the other says that the runners dress like the butchers who began this tradition.

When Hemingway first came to Pamplona in 1923, before popularizing this festival in *The Sun Also Rises*, only the Basques and the Spanish came. Now half the crowd comes from all over Europe and from points across the world.

Photo shops along the plaza would soon have photos of the run. They put prints up on boards, and people spend hours looking for themselves in the *encierro* and will buy prints when they find their tragic expressions.

My new friend was taken away by a crowd of arm-in-arm men and women from his peña. He shouted he'd be at the Windsor all day and that he expected that drink.

I spotted Juan Macho, my guide to this misunderstood festival, and his crowd of veteran runners at the Bar Txoko up in a corner of the main plaza. Juan is a jolly little Cuban who becomes fierce when he tightens his eyes. He has the physique of Anthony Hopkins and a bearing that shifts from sage to matador in a blink of his brown-gray eyes. He has a gray goa-tee and most of his silver-streaked hair and a walk that says he's a self-made man who has burned out his angst and now is at peace with himself. He is in his late sixties now, and each year he takes a few wards to Pamplona to show them the depths of the festival. He keeps running each year to stay in touch with his mortality and his manliness. Now he typically runs the "suicide run," the beginning of the course where a few runners sprint directly at the bulls before dodging to the side of the street. He doesn't run every day anymore. He is transitioning to retirement. In his silver years he prefers to teach. His old knees now protest his runs toward bulls. He has seen many injured in the run because they didn't know how to run. He wants to help those he can.

Juan was born in Cuba and emigrated to the United States when he was twelve years old. He has taught college courses on Latin America and spent much of his career as a consultant for American companies looking to invest in Central America, Caribbean nations, or South American countries. He first came to Pamplona because, like most, he was drawn to the party. He ran with the bulls and learned something about himself. This something began to straighten out his life. He began living more boldly, more honestly, with more purpose. He found running somehow made him a better man. He went back. He met many of the great runners and learned from them. He felt stronger and his eyes opened. This running, this facing your mortality along with bulls—beasts that are 1,200 pounds of muscle and power that will probably die before an audience that day at the hands of bull-fighters who might very well die, too—tapped into something, some essence of his life. But that wasn't enough. He'd sipped this brew of manliness and wanted more. He wanted to understand it, not just swim in its testosterone, as so many do at the San Fermín festival. He began to read and to visit with Basques who knew the history. He found there are religious depths to the San Fermín festival. San Fermín is, after all, a Catholic saint in a very Catholic country. He found Hemingway understood this and used this to create the characters he did. Juan joined the Hemingway Society and continued to investigate and learn.

I saw Juan standing outside the Bar Txoko in the bright morning sun drinking a Kaiku with brandy from a plastic cup with many others. He looked at me and nodded solemnly as he said loudly, "Now you've glimpsed your mortality." As he said this, he handed me some churro, rounded sticks of fried dough covered in sugar. This pastry is made each morning in a Basque bakery where men churn flour in an ancient cauldron according to a medieval recipe.

I asked, "Where were you? You said you'd run with me."

"Yes," he replied with devilish calm, "it's better to run alone your first time, as we face our mortality alone."

A dozen veteran bull runners laughed at me and then with me. A tremendous man named Tony, a construction worker from Queens who had this wonderfully profane New York working man manner of speaking, bellowed, "Just before the bulls were on you I saw your fuckin' face twisted up like the fuckin' Reaper just found your ass. Wish I had a fuckin' photo."

The veteran runners were laughing with me and Juan leaned close and said, "Remember, you're just beginning."

As I looked at Juan and the diverse group that makes up his peña, I saw that when you pursue an icon, as the Hemingway man surely is, you go down a rabbit hole into something unexpected, something designed to rip down your ego and send you packing if you can't handle what's to come. Sure, you know basically what is going to happen—in this case, that bulls would be coming—but not how it would feel and if you can take it and if you want to keep taking it. You stand up to it by degrees. You become addicted to the rush, even the fear. Or maybe you don't. Maybe it's not for you. Or maybe you fail and become Francis Macomber. If you do, you'll have to redeem yourself like he did in that jarring story about a man learning to stand up and be a man. Or you can live on with a secret hole right through your manhood. It's up to you.

Most people, of course, only run with the bulls once. It's a thrill. They check it off their bucket list and go on about their lives not much changed at all. Though a profound experience, that's not a rite of passage. It's only a validation of being alive and that you have some balls. One morning, this darling little American college girl with curly blonde hair clomped by me in the crowded street minutes before the bulls would come. She was wearing rubber boots many sizes too large for her little feet. Someone pointed at her boots and shouted, "You can't run in those." She yelled back with this little-girl spite crinkling her cute nose, "I didn't know I was going to do this, so I don't have anything else to wear." She was probably backpacking Europe on the wings of one of her parents' credit card. She found herself in Pamplona, and when everyone at the bars said they were going to run, she followed along on the slippery slope of peer pressure. Her heels or who knows what just wouldn't do, so someone gave her the boots. She probably made it through the run unscathed by clinging to the side of the street with so many others, but to call what she did a rite of passage is to mock the whole thing. She likely learned nothing. She didn't respect the ritual and wasn't trying to understand. She was only following peer pressure into something dangerous. Now she has an adorable tale for cocktail parties.

The men, and a few women, I met after my first run view running with the bulls as something more. They want to be in sync with the running bulls in the moving crowd. They are driven to come back again and again for the fleeting connection of wild moments on the edge. They keep coming back because something is alive in the San Fermín festival that is difficult to find anywhere else after the trials of youth have passed. This rite of passage isn't as obvious as three months in boot camp but is no less real when taken with eyes and mind open.

As I met the people in Juan's peña, I found they were of different backgrounds and ages and that some were rich and others poor and that this didn't matter. There was a plumber from Lowell, Massachusetts, who was only there his second time but had come back with a massive tattoo of a black fighting bull on his right arm. There was a gray-haired Hollywood producer who was on his thirtieth year who told me, "Those not living on the edge are taking up too much room." There was a white-haired homebuilder from Atlanta named Richard who told me, "My wife says Pamplona is cheaper than therapy." There was a heart surgeon, J. J., who has become the charismatic leader of Juan's peña. When I asked where he'd gotten a silver pin of a fighting bull he had pinned on his bandana, he replied, "I earned it. This was bestowed on me by Basques in a very exclusive peña." I nodded respect.

There was this happy spark lighting all their eyes that has something to do with the want for a party, but also for the search for a tangible meaning—for what Hemingway called the "authentic life." None of them say this. When I ask why they keep coming back, they tell me to see their amigos. Honest enough, but true friends are always made by shared experience—friendships become stale and end when the something in common (school, a job, a hobby, or running on the horns) ends. That something in common is why they're really in Pamplona. That something has everything to do with life, as Somerset Maugham put it, on the razor's edge.

It wasn't always this way.

Before *The Sun Also Rises* was published in 1926, in a 1923 story for the *Toronto Star Weekly*, Hemingway witnessed the run for the first time and treated it as an example of extreme sportsmanship. He said the run with the bulls "is the Pamplona tradition of giving the bulls a final shot at everyone in town before they enter the pens. They will not leave until they come out into the glare of the arena to die in the afternoon." This was only his first impression.

Hemingway likely never ran with the bulls. He never claimed to have gotten into the street to run with the bulls, and Hemingway wasn't above boasting or even purposely stoking a true anecdote into a flamboyant lie if it added to the Hemingway-man persona. Hemingway boasted he'd had sex with the gorgeous girlfriend of the notorious gangster, Legs Diamond, outside the 21 Club in New York City. He claimed that he threw an African lion out of Harry's New York Bar in Paris. He told his friend and biographer A. E. Hotchner that he married an eighteen-year-old Wakamba girl named Debba while on safari with his fourth wife, Mary. He said he slept with Mary and Debba on a goatskin fourteen feet wide. Hotchner couldn't find anything to substantiate this or the other tales. Hemingway claimed to have "fucked very well" a World War I spy named Mata Hari, but Hotchner writes "such an encounter could not possibly have taken place since Mati Hari had been executed by the French in 1917 and Hemingway had first gone abroad in 1918 as a Red Cross ambulance driver in Italy."[2]

Such boasting led James Michener to write that "Hemingway's whole public life was dedicated to the creation of a legend."[3]

That certainly has truth in it, but Hemingway wanted to be judged at the end as a writer. In a 1950 letter to Robert Cantwell, Hemingway wrote: "I asked both Cape and Scribners not to use any publicity about any military service and it is distasteful to me to mention it and destroys any pride I have in it. I want to run as a writer; not as a man who had been to the wars; nor a bar room fighter; nor a shooter; nor a horse-player; nor a drinker. I would like to be a straight writer and be judged as such. . . ."

What Hemingway did do was get into the arena with the *vaquillas*—cows with leather on their horns. After the bulls run up the streets and into the arena, the bulls are herded out of the bullfighting arena in view of a packed stadium. The fighting bulls will be held in the dark by themselves until they'll run back into the arena in the afternoon to fight and die. But when the bulls leave, it's not over for the runners who have run into the arena. The door at the entrance to the Plaza de Toros will be closed, and *vaquillas*, cows with leather on their horns,

---

[2] A. E. Hotchner, *Papa Hemingway*, Carroll and Graf, New York, 1955.
[3] James Michener, *Iberia*, Dial Press, New York, 1968.

will be released into arena with the runners. Hemingway called this spectacle "the amateurs," as some of the runners would use their shirts or other improvised capes to attempt passes with the *vaquillas*. But these cows are not new to bullfighting, as the fighting bulls are. These cows have learned how to aim for the person, not the cape. Hemingway, and some of his companions, did get into the arena to play with the *vaquillas*. Hemingway even boasted they became crowd favorites.

Still, despite all the hyperbole, and even if Hemingway never ran with the bulls, Hemingway's image has become entwined with the people wearing white clothes and red sashes and bandanas during the San Fermín festival and with the people who run with fighting bulls. Though he likely didn't step into the street with fighting bulls, nor did his character Jake in *The Sun Also Rises*, they are still stirred into the mystery of its rituals.

So went my first run in 2007, and I thought it was the rite of passage until it was done, then I knew it was only the first terror and confusion. Not being in control of what is happening but nevertheless being caught in the roar of all its heady rapture is the confusion. Being under the power of something else, something you can't reason with and that can hurt you very badly, is the terror. Learning to suspend your imagination and keep your head when all others are losing theirs, as Rudyard Kipling said in his perfect poem "If," is what the Hemingway man requires.

All this had happened before. Decades ago, just after my head had been shaved to stubble, a drill sergeant gave me his first go at tearing down my ego, and I thought that was the rite of passage. The first time I'd belayed off a cliff and had to jump for a hold to climb back up, I again thought that was the rite of passage and that everything would change after that first terror and confusion. The first time I stepped into a boxing ring with a professional fighter who'd been told to see if I could take a punch—and so would be worth training—I also thought that must be the rite of passage. Now I know these jarring trials are simply the first explosive and ego-humbling step of a real rite of passage to becoming all we want to be.

Actually, thinking of a first run with the bulls as a rite of passage is like thinking of a first beer as a rite of passage. Maybe it is in modern parlance, but it's not the full ancient rite of man addressed in this book. A first beer or a first time behind the wheel is a first step into a rite, but there is so much more to it than this exciting first experience. Drinking, after all, isn't manly. Knowing how much to drink, and not to drink, is manly. Driving isn't manly. Driving well is manly. Not understanding this is a large part of the reason for the state of so many of today's men.

Realizing that the terror and the confusion is only the first step opens you up to the dimension a true rite of passage presents—to the rites developed and honed by Spartans, Apaches, Samurai, and every other group, tribe, nation, or organization that knew or knows that men who can be counted on must be built; that the safety and future of their tribe, army, organization, or club can't be left to chance; that men must be humbled and then emboldened as they are fused to the code of values of the group.

So I'd been rattled and would be again, but these men were laughing and their eyes were wide open and their voices alive.

These men who'd each run a hundred times or more with the bulls and were drawn back every year to this festival and its *encierro* were the officers, and I was a mere recruit.

This was the beginning, not the end. That realization drew me back into the street on following days and back again in 2013 for a deeper investigation of the Hemingway man with the group going from Paris to Pamplona. We'd traveled by trains to San Sebastian, Spain. We spent the night in that port city before driving in a rented van over pine green mountains to Pamplona the following day to run with the bulls and where I'd enter a fraternity of runners living this part of the Hemingway man no one has ever explained.

I knew my terror and confusion in this rite of passage had passed, but I was about to find that the real trouble was ahead and always present. Confronting what you're afraid of to become a more confident man is what the terror and confusion portion of a rite of passage is about, but next comes the gauntlet, which leads to more profound things.

I saw this from a different vantage on my first day back in Pamplona in 2013, before the first run of the bulls in the festival. Juan and I walked in the midday sun over a small bridge to where the fighting bulls are held in corrals enclosed in a building. You must pay five euros to see them. We did and looked through Plexiglas windows at the bulls lying placidly with steers to keep them calm. Later in the evening, the six of these bulls that would fight the next day would be driven down a winding, barely-two-lane road and across a bridge over a brown river to a pen the size of an average American's living room. There they'd wait under guard until they'd be driven up the streets at 8:00 a.m. with all the people to the arena.

Seeing them there in a sort of zoo before they'd run together and perhaps hurt or even kill people and before they'd find themselves alone in the arena in the afternoon was humbling and sad. It reminded me of the hunt, which is always both exciting and humbling and, when you kill, melancholy. All that is very primal and honest if you hunt ethically and respect and eat what you kill, but is also hard to explain to anyone who has never taken the responsibility of killing their own meat, or at least raising their own vegetables and therefore being forced to defend their sustenance from deer, rabbits, birds, and insects—from reality.

I told Juan this, and he explained that the running of the bulls and the bullfight grew from the Coliseum, yes, but before that from the hunt. It is a throwback to when men had to slay dangerous beasts for meat. The Romans, and for centuries after, the Spanish, fought bulls from horseback with spears. This was but a step away from what hunters did on horseback. Hunters, on foot or on horseback, used brutal and primitive weapons to kill big game. As they did, they had to master themselves as they stalked animals that might, if not killed cleanly, come and destroy them.

Juan said simply, "The run with the bulls and the bullfight is this ancient reality ritualized into a tragedy."

This primal reality is also the reason the Hemingway man is a hunter. Juan doesn't hunt, but I do. I told him how I've found that after the kill, the animal loses its dignity. The only dignity it has then is the respect we give it. People have lost touch with this today because they don't have to kill to eat. Still, if a hunter abuses a dead animal or wastes the meat it gave with its life, he has disrespected himself and his natural connection. As we walked back up to the singing streets of Pamplona, I told Juan about how these primal experiences in Pamplona are like a few things I'd undergone just weeks before in Africa.

We had driven through the South African bush and the long green grass filling in the ground beneath thorn bush and acacia trees in Kruger National Park. We stopped in a clearing on the west side of a small hill looking into the setting sun. We stepped out alongside an off-road bus to have what Africans call a sundowner, a beer, as we watched the day end. I was with a few writers, a ranger whose job it was to catch or kill rhino poachers, the president of the South African Wildlife College, and a professor who'd spent his career as a game ranger but was then teaching a dozen students how to be licensed professional hunters (PH).

As we drank beer and listened to the ranger tell stories about rhino poachers, three elephants, all immature bulls in their twenties, began feeding up the slope toward us. We were laughing and speaking loudly, but the elephants, which aren't legally hunted there, didn't seem to mind. When the elephants closed to 100 feet, the game ranger said, "They won't bother us. They know we're here. They approached us."

A minute after the ranger said this, the closest bull elephant stopped, and all the muscles under his gray skin stiffened. One of the elephant's rear feet actually froze in the air. Something had disturbed the bull. The bull was broadside to us. He was close enough for us to see the creases in his gray hide and to see the black eyelashes over his right brown eye. Then all that went blurry.

The bull broke from his frozen stance. He was coming. He turned his tons of flesh and bone toward us and charged with his ears out and his head high. He covered ground fast before he used his yellowed tusks to bulldoze over a small tree. The tree cracked and crashed into the grass. The bull stopped as dust washed over his long gray legs. When he stopped his charge, he raised his trunk and head as high as he could. He towered over us and he knew it. He looked down at us from the bottoms of his eye sockets. He was so close, I was looking up into his brown eyes.

I was standing next to the ranger and everyone was behind us. After a moment I wish I had a video of, the ranger took off his hat and shook it at the bull while shouting, "Get outta here!"

The bull flinched like a dog someone is trying to kick and moved quickly off with the others and it was over.

The ranger had adrenaline reddening his face as he said, "That's often how it is. I've had many of my closest calls just feet from the truck. Damn, I should have had my rifle."

As my blood cooled, I asked how many times he'd been charged, and he said he really didn't know. He said hippos kill the most people, but they mostly do that at night when they leave the rivers to feed. He said Cape buffalo scare him the most. He said with elephants they'll usually warn you. Rhinos don't warn you, but they mostly run away, and when they charge it's almost always a bluff. He told us some stories about lions charging and elephants he had to stop with his rifle, and as we listened to this ranger in worn khakis and a leather fedora, a man who had so much experience with wildlife and hunting men who poach white and black rhino, we knew he was a Hemingway man all right.

We spent the next day at the South African Wildlife College and found a terror and confusion portion of a rite of passage few people believe when I tell them. A dozen students were there to take a course on becoming a PH. They were learning to track game, to shoot, to assess trophy size of wild-life, to survive in the bush, to deal with poachers, and other such things.

Only two of the dozen students taking the eighteen-month course were white. The rest were black and one was a black woman, but they all wanted to be the PH-ideal Hemingway had once written so much about, an icon played by men like Gregory Peck, Clark Gable, and Stewart Granger. Hemingway called the men who played this part "white hunters," but like the best ideals, this one is growing according to honest values and so is dropping ethnicity and even gender from its definition.

I found that the terror and confusion in their rite of passage was something much fiercer than stepping into a crowded street to run with fighting bulls. These college-aged students had to stalk within twenty yards of dangerous game in Kruger National Park—rhino, elephant, lion, hippo, and Cape buffalo. And then they had to slip away unseen, know-ing that at those distances a shift in the wind could bring an elephant or lion charging with death in its eyes. To do this, they had to master their fear as they learned to move quietly and to read sign and the body language of wildlife. They also had to learn to kill wildlife if they had to defend their life or that of others with them.

Stalking dangerous game wasn't even their real terror. They also had to sit blindfolded by a watering hole where lions, hyenas, elephants, and more come to drink. They had to sit blindfolded for hours alongside rivers alive with croco-diles and hippos. Somewhere out of earshot their professor, a retired game ranger, was watching with a rifle, but that wasn't much comfort.

They had to sit for hours using their ears and noses to detect what was around them. One twenty-year-old student said to me, "It's deathly frightening, but you feel so alive. You start to smell things you didn't know you could. You hear things and sort them out in ways you didn't know you could. The primal fear sharpens you. There is nothing more terrifying than being certain you hear a leopard or a lion close and coming. But still you have to keep control. Running would only trigger a predatory response. You have to master the fear to pass this part of the course."

All of the students in the course told me that sitting blindfolded on the bare ground where predators come to drink made them realize how serious what they were trying to do is. All of them said the terror made them feel alive and intensely ready for what would come next in their course.

This is what the terror and the confusion does in a real rite of passage, but it's only the beginning. The things that would come next as I chased the Hemingway man were much more memorable than fear.

STEP 3

The Guides

Aside from a handful of guys, boxing is missing the good train-ers, that's why our sport is so in the air now because we don't have people who have the capability to not only train fighters but also train and create decent respectable citizens of the world.

—Alexis Arguello, a three-time world champion boxer

ON THE MORNING OF THE sixth day of July, Juan Macho put on a white outfit complete with a white cap and lab coat. He stood in the sunlight filtering through large win-dows and doors that open to a small fourth-floor balcony in the ancient part of Pamplona. Juan had left his Borsalino Panama hat with his linen jacket and the rest of the summer outfits he'd worn in Paris packed away and put on this white suit that reminded me of something house painters once wore.

57

I began laughing at Juan and asking if he was planning to brighten up the apartment's white walls to get a better rate on the rent.

He looked at me with his matador-serious eyes and said, "Wait and see, my young ward."

We went down the flights of stairs to the narrow and bright streets. We followed a stream of happy people to a sunlit plaza in late morning. Everyone was in white and red and had the joy of people expecting a party on their faces and in their strides.

We found spots to stand along the base of a building in the mayor's plaza. In a few hours, the Chupinazo would take place. This is where the festival begins at noon on July 6 every year. After this, the bulls run for eight days straight, then the people pack into this plaza again to sing *"Pobre de Mí, Pobre de Mí, que se han acabado las fiestas, de San Fermín."* (Poor me, poor me, for the fiesta of San Fermín has come to a close.)

On this first day of the fiesta, people kept pushing into the oblong square. The plaza is about half the size of a football field, and people were pushing in from streets on every point of the compass. A Japanese couple was in front of me, and a German built like a professional rugby player was on my right. Many around us were Spanish or Basque, but there were people from every country in Europe and many beyond. Long before noon, we learned how people are crushed to death by panicked crowds. We fought to breathe and looked up the many colored buildings to the people on the balconies pouring wine on us and to the blue sky above them.

Beach balls were bouncing on outstretched hands of a crowd moving in convulsions. People became packed so tight, we didn't fall down even when we lost our footing.

It was like being held up by your elbows and shoulders and being tossed about with no control. It was like trying to catch your breath in a mosh pit at a heavy metal concert.

When the mayor finally appeared on his balcony, people gasped from relief. He had children and women in dresses around him smiling. It was hard to pick him out from all the waving people on the building's many ornate balconies.

When they noticed the moment was upon them, everyone on the packed plaza took off their red bandanas and held them toward the mayor, which turned the turbulent sea of people bright red. After a lot of Spanish flair on that blue-sky day, the mayor set off a rocket. A roar went up from the crowd. This was like a spark igniting the city. People poured wine from the many balconies over the narrow streets, and all the people below were soon bright red.

I was drenched with red wine and was so beaten up, my ribs would hurt for days; but Juan, through all this, stood with his arms crossed over his chest pushing back with his elbows as the crush of people moved and broke like ocean water on a sea wall. He had his eyes closed most of the time and looked as calm as a man lying under a shady tree. Some people idiotically tried to dodge the wine and sangria; others reveled in the coronation; Juan was simply at peace with the mad scene.

As the crowd began to break, Juan opened his eyes and smiled as he said, "And so it begins."

***

We fell out of the crowd. They were streaming to the pubs. We went back to the apartment and changed into bright white clothes. We were going to something more somber.

Juan said, "Come, we have to pay homage to the fallen."

As he said this, he carefully tied his red bandana around his neck with a slipknot. The veteran runners use slipknots because a few runners have had their bandanas hooked by a fighting bull's forward-facing horns. They were dragged along the stones streets until the frustrated bull paused to ravage them.

Juan was then dressed in a fine white shirt and washed-out red sash and bandanna with emblems of his peña stitched in and knots tied in the tassels of his sash, one for each run with the bulls—over eighty in all. I only had three then and would have more in the coming days, but now it was time to say good-bye to fallen runners and to pray for safe runs and bullfights.

We went back down to the singing streets of Pamplona during a San Fermín festival. The July afternoon was warm and the mountain sun bright. The narrow streets wended in front of us and beneath stone buildings. Many small steel balconies were above. Some were flapping with drying laundry. Others had people leaning over them in clear and warm afternoon air with glasses of wine in their hands and smiles on their voices. There was music echoing everywhere. Some was traditional folk, but also every other tune that a drum or brass instrument could smash or blow seemed to be playing.

A peña's band just passed. Behind it were people who follow these bands all over the city. We passed a small square with six wooden picnic tables. People in bright white clothes were eating *chorizo*, a thick Spanish pork sausage, as a half dozen children chased one another with squirt guns. A small brass band led by a saxophonist was playing in the cool shade growing along the north and west edges of the small plaza.

We walked a few more blocks along San Francisco Street to the side entrance of the San Lorenzo church. Inside is the Chapel of San Fermín, opening from one side as a large, adjacent hall. This chapel was completed in 1717. A wedding was just finishing in the main church, and the bride and groom were going out the main entrance opposite us under waves of confetti and music from a choir in robes.

We passed through the jubilant crowd in the church and turned left into the chapel. Most of the seats on the wooden pews were taken. Behind the altar of the chapel was the carved wooden statue of San Fermín, the saint this festival is centered around. This ancient statue is life-size and sits on an ornate throne. The statue wears a red and gold robe, holds a golden staff, and is crowned with a tall hat shining from gold thread.

San Fermín might have been real, but if so, his true story has been lost and has risen again within folklore. Legend has it that there was a senator, Firmus, who lived in the time of the Roman emperors Diocleciano and Maximiano and was the governor of this region of Spain. This senator had a son named Fermín. These facts come from Jacobo de Voragine, under the title "The Golden Legend," which dates from 1254. According to this legend, Firmus sent his son to be educated by a priest, Saint Honestus. This priest eventually asked an archbishop to ordain Fermín to make him a missionary. This was done, and Fermín later returned to Pamplona as a bishop. Later, while traveling as a missionary in Amiens, France, according to the legend, Fermín managed to convert around three thousand people to Christianity in only forty days. This disturbed the local Roman governor. Fermín was arrested and murdered in jail—making him a Christian martyr. Many historians have looked into this account and have found it to be a legend grown over generations.

The legend arrived in Pamplona for the first time during the twelfth century. The archbishop of Pamplona, Pedro de Paris, heard it and had a relic brought to the Cathedral de Pamplona and placed it on the altar. For the people of Pamplona at that time, the idea that they had a saint who had once been a bishop from their town was something to be valued. Over time, they started to adorn the legend to include the Christianization of their own town in the first century, instead of the third century, as the people from Amiens dated it. Over the following years, different scribes enlarged and modified the original legend.

Meanwhile, though San Fermín is the patron saint of this fiesta, the celebration began in two different medieval events. Commercial fairs were traditionally held at the beginning of the summer, when cattle merchants would come into town with their animals. In the fourteenth century, bullfighting became a part of the tradition. Meanwhile, religious ceremonies honoring San Fermín were held in October. But then, in 1591, this religious celebration was transferred to July 7 to take place at the same time as the fair. This is considered to be the beginning of the "Sanfermines." During medieval times, this fiesta included an opening speech, musicians, tournaments, theatre, bullfights, dances, and even fireworks. Bull running began in the seventeenth and eighteenth centuries after some began to test their courage with the bulls as they were taken to the arena.

Since 1591, the key date of the festival has been July 7, as this is when thousands of people accompany the fifteenth-century statue of Saint Fermín through the old city of Pamplona. Dancers, street entertainers, and different political and religious authorities fill the parade. During the procession, a *jota* (an ancient traditional dance) is performed for the saint, and the *gigantes* (enormous wood-framed and papier-mâché puppet figures worn by performers) dance and twirl while the cathedral bell named María rings over the city.

All that would happen the next day. On this day, in front of the altar and that ancient statue of San Fermín that would be carried through the city, there were three poster-sized prints of American men who had passed away during the previous year. Each had come to Pamplona many times and was known by everyone in the room. The photos showed each wearing the San Fermín colors with the light of the fiesta in their eyes.

Juan and I took two of the last seats, and soon foreign bull runners were filling the aisles. The priest stepped onto the altar flanked by altar boys in black robes and white cassocks. The parish priest of this church is always the chairman of the board of the Corte de San Fermín, a religious association set up in 1885 to use the legend of San Fermín as a guide for this festival. The priest turned away from us and raised his palms to the statue of San Fermín behind the altar. He began the Mass. Later, during his homily, the priest blessed the runners and prayed for their safety and said, "When we run on the horns we run with a saint. Life is meant to be run with the knowledge we are mortal and that we must face our mortality with God, as good moral men and women. Those who run with life and knowledge run with God."

As I looked around the chapel and back to the saint, I wondered if Hemingway knew all he'd popularized. Hemingway had come to this chapel. He also sent his character Jake here. In the novel, Jake comes to this chapel and prays for everybody he can think of. He prays for Lady Brett and for a good outcome for the trip, and he prays for Robert Cohn. He prays for the bullfights, the fiesta, and for the fishing he would do before the fiesta. By praying for Robert and everyone, Jake follows the Catholic guidelines for prayer, as Catholics are instructed to pray "for all, without exception, in high or low station, for the just, for sinners, for infidels. . . ." Harry "Stoney" Stoneback said, "The novel's rituals seen in the church and the bullfights delineate precisely the values that give meaning to life and death (passion, honor, courage, decorum, aesthetics, and morality, for a start). These values are the bedrock of *The Sun Also Rises*."

Those values are more felt than stated in the novel. Nevertheless, they are the foundation of the Hemingway man. So I also prayed for safe runs and clean bullfights and for everyone looking at all of this from their own points of view. I stopped there and pondered as a choir sang and the priest gave the Mass. Jake's mind also wandered during his prayer for everybody, and he felt rotten about it. He felt unworthy of what Hemingway called "a grand religion." Some critics have used this feeling to draw the conclusion that Jake was falling away from the church as a member of the "Lost Generation." They argue that Jake is emblematic of the erosion of the old values built on the bedrock of Christianity and say this points to the weakness of church doctrine. I find that such critics are projecting their own misunderstanding of prayer.

Stoney says that "in the presence of what Jake calls the 'grandeur' of church how can he feel anything but unworthy? Suppose he had said, 'I was proud I was such a great Catholic.' Would any good Catholic say that? His fundamental stance here is reflected in the words of the familiar prayer, the *Domine, non sum dignus*: 'Lord, I am not worthy . . . but only say the word and I shall be healed.'"

Actually, in this scene Jake is a great deal like Hemingway. Shortly after *The Sun Also Rises* was published, Hemingway wrote in letters to friends that he "was a very dumb Catholic" but he had "so much faith" that he "hated to examine into it." He also said the only way he "could run his life decently was to accept the discipline of the Church."

As I looked at all the different faces in the chapel—from so many different lands—I thought that without a guide I would have gone to Mass, as I am a practicing Catholic, but I wouldn't have been part of this Mass for fallen runners. I would have missed all this, as many have missed much in Hemingway.

Still, Juan is a devious guide. He showed me this scene but stayed out of my way. After pondering this, I realize the greatest guides are keepers of the myths, the stories that transport us from what we can know to what we can only perceive. True guides are enforcers and icons. To be iconic, they need to stand back and correct wrongs, but to otherwise keep opinions to themselves. They need to stay out of the way of the rite of passage and to be emblematic of its rituals. This is what Jake had done in the novel, and this is what Juan was doing for me. This is why a drill instructor can be loud and intense, but nevertheless won't do a lot of explaining. He is there to show the way. He represents an ideal. He is there to make corrections. He should never let it become personal. Like a coach, he must watch his men and/or women and show by example. Explaining too much would force a guide to relate. To do this, they'd have to give anecdotes and points of view. These things are human and based on context and can easily be misunderstood, as different people have their own experiences and ways of seeing, understanding the same things. Such is why good guides stand back when they can and try to be iconic and mysterious. After all, if the mystery is lost, the icon they're representing is lost and the person, in all their biases and failings, is all that's left. This is why the legend of San Fermín is ideal for this complex and often misunderstood festival, as the loose mythology defining San Fermín is pliable enough to bring experiences together within the rituals grown here.

I think this is why Jake says very little about why they're on the journey in *The Sun Also Rises*. I also think this is why this novel still grabs so many.

✳✳✳

After the service for lost runners, we spilled out of the chapel and into warm afternoon sun. We were still in the melancholy contemplation of the service, so we opted to walk up the crowded streets and across the sun-drenched central plaza to the bronze statue of Papa Hemingway outside the Plaza de Toros.

The statue is under the shade of towering Spanish oaks outside the coliseum-shaped arena. In the street party of a festival, people had left red empty plastic cups at the base of the statue. Out of respect, someone had climbed the statue and tied a red handkerchief around Hemingway's bronze neck. There were people lying in the shade of the oaks on the bright day with their heads spinning from a day in the bars.

We stopped under the statue's large bronze head and toasted Hemingway. We asked him in jest why he never ran and decided that perhaps Hemingway and his lead man, Jake, didn't need to run. They'd proven themselves already and so could watch a boxing match or a bullfight and relate to the mortal struggle. They knew what is needed from inside a man because they'd been tested and bloodied in something much more serious than running with fighting bulls. Jake (and Hemingway) had been wounded in battle in World War I. They could observe and understand without testing themselves in the terror and confusion of being in the street with bulls that matadors would kill or maybe be killed by.

Running with the bulls, we conceded, is really very silly anyway. It's real and has depth if you take it that way, but it is about man's need to test himself, and that can look absurd when on public display. Hemingway deepens the sensation of absurdity by having Jake witness a Spaniard being killed by a bull just where the run narrows as it enters the arena. Jake then goes to a café and discusses this man's brutal end with a waiter. The waiter says, "You hear? *Muerto*. Dead. He's dead. With a horn through him. All for morning fun. *Es muy flamenco.*"

Jake politely withholds his opinion. He is always careful about issuing judgments. He doesn't like to make simple pronouncements about complicated things or about things he just doesn't know about yet.

That afternoon, Pedro Romero, a fictional bullfighter who appears in the novel and falls for Lady Brett, kills this *muerto* bull so well, the judges present him with one of its ears. Romero makes a show of giving the bloody ear to Lady Brett with the whole arena watching. Brett, Hemingway tells us, "wrapped it in a handkerchief belonging to myself [Jake] and left both ear and handkerchief, along with a number of Muratti cigarette stubs, shoved far back in the drawer of the bed-table that stood beside her bed in the Hotel Montoya, in Pamplona."

The ear left to rot with cigarette butts gasps of senselessness. The loss of life of both the Spanish runner—who Hemingway tells us was a husband and father—and of the bull seems dirty after all the manly excitement of the run and the bullfight. Only Romero, the young and honorable bullfighter, is left standing tall in his tight and sparkling bullfighting suit. But then in Romero's wake is death and butcher shops for the bulls and maybe one day he'll be killed in the arena, too. Those things seem obvious to a modern reader, but there is more Hemingway alluded to that's often overlooked.

Brett left the ear to rot. She could have thrown it to the crowd or buried it with a prayer of thanks or at least have given it a respectful thank-you as she laid it in a trash can. Instead, she disrespects the ear and with it the bull and herself. She hides it away where a chambermaid will find it stinking and toss it while cursing or holding her breath. She let it become something vile. It wasn't vile on the bull. It wasn't vile as a gift according to the ancient Spanish rituals. Romero didn't see it as anything but celebratory. It was turned into something vile by her apathy for it and for herself. If Brett had run with the bulls or had found some way to understand and respect the bulls, and through them herself, she would have treated the ear more compassionately.

In the novel, Brett runs off with men frivolously and tosses them away when she's bored. She takes no responsibility for her actions and for their destruction. Robert Cohn is left wandering aimlessly after her. Though he'll likely recover, even Romero is ruined by her. No, the ear left in the drawer wasn't a simple declaration that running with and killing bulls is senseless. Hemingway loved bullfights. In 1923, Hemingway wrote in an article for the *Toronto Star Weekly*: "I am not going to apologise for bull fighting. It is a survival of the days of the Roman Coliseum. But it does need some explanation. Bull fighting is not a sport. It was never supposed to be. It is a tragedy. A very great tragedy. The tragedy is the death of the bull. It is played in three definite acts." He wasn't condemning bullfighting or running. Rather, the rotting ear is a metaphor for Brett's meaningless life. Her favorite saying was "what rot," and that is what the ear was doing and that is what she was doing with her life. She could hurt the men who didn't understand this. She could hurt the others, too, but their wounds weren't gaping.

Hemingway was giving us something deeper than a simple declaration that the run and the death of the bulls are meaningless. The rituals in this fiesta are real, and without the bulls and even the death of the bulls it would lose its meaning. So much of this reality is hidden from us today. So we must not come to simpleminded conclusions; we must withhold judgment as we try to understand, as Jake did.

Only such an introspective undertaking could have saved Brett. Her life was rotting because she wasn't living it honestly, authentically, and with accountability. She was behaving selfishly and dishonestly. She had redeeming qualities, but until she respected herself, she'd continue to destroy herself and those around her. To begin her reformation, all she had to do was respect that bloody bull's ear and through it the life the bull gave.

Brett, though, is an unfinished character. She's supposed to be. The story wasn't about her. She was a catalyst for showing what an ass a juvenile man like Robert Cohn can be when he meets a seductive woman who doesn't take responsibility for her actions. Brett was there to round out the characters Robert and Jake. This isn't how many feminists have seen it. Rena Sanderson, author of *Hemingway's Italy*, said Hemingway's fiction divided women into "castrators or love-slaves." Nina Baym, author of *Women's Fiction*, argued that Brett Ashley and Margot Macomber "are the two outstanding examples of Hemingway's 'bitch women.'" From the 1960s to today, feminists have seen Hemingway as an enemy of women. What they're missing is that Hemingway's often-simplistic female characters are there to tell us something about men, not women. The critiques that argue Hemingway's women characters are "love-slaves" or "bitch women" are actually saying more about their view of men than about Hemingway.

To avoid such fairer-sex bewilderments, most ritualized rites of passage designed to turn boys into men separate boys from the ladies. Because most boys are attracted to and confused by girls, boot camp and football camp mostly separate boys from girls. Most ancient coming-of-age rituals did this, too. The Maasai's *Enkipaata* (pre-circumcision ceremony) groups boys from ages fourteen to sixteen years together and takes them from their mothers. They travel about the tribe's lands in a group. Through a series of ceremonies and trials, the Maasai boys advance toward manhood with men who'd earned the status of elders as guides and enforcers of the rituals.

This Spanish rite of passage, however, now has women as participants and bystanders. Women weren't allowed to run in Hemingway's day, but now they are and some do. This hasn't weakened the rite of passage, but it has made it modern.

Hemingway actually wrote in *The Dangerous Summer* (experienced in 1959, decades after his novel popularized this festival) that Pamplona's festival is "a man's fiesta and women at it make trouble, never intentionally of course, but they nearly always make or have trouble." Brett was present in *The Sun Also Rises* just for this reason. She was there to show more clearly the difference between Robert Cohn and Jake Barnes. Without her in the novel, we wouldn't have as clear a picture of the Hemingway man.

Juan and I pondered these changes as we left the Hemingway statue in the shade of the Spanish oaks outside the bullfighting arena in midafternoon. We wandered down Estafeta, a street where the bulls run but that at this time of the day was filled with happy bar-hopping people.

A group of Spanish young women with their white shirts stained red from wine poured over them passed us. Juan looked at them and said, "It's good that some women run with the bulls now."

"Good?" I said. "Funny, I thought of you as a purist."

He shook his head as we continued to shoulder through the street party. He placed his hand on my shoulder, and we stopped in the moving crowd as he said, "Until the feminists begin to help these young women understand why they run and what they're trying to become—that a woman can be brave and honorable and feminine—the feminists will be stopped in time."

This thought made me want to buy him a drink. It is too rich. I asked, "You're saying the feminists' dislike of the Hemingway man is based on a misunderstanding they need to resolve about themselves?"

"And it's a shame," said Juan as we continued to walk down the center of Estafeta. I asked, "So you're saying that today's feminists attack conservative women because they think a woman who is both strong and a lady has agreed to take part in some man-centric role-play game?"

Juan nodded and said, "I'd put it this way. Modern feminists who see such strong women as sellouts need to create a more honest ideal. They need to stop blaming men. Men are no longer the problem. It's their icon that is?"

Another group of twenty-something Spanish ladies in white slacks and red shirts turned in front of us from a side street of the ancient part of the city. Most of them were wearing heels, but they were all in clothes they could toss away after the fiesta. They were singing a Spanish tune and laughing and swaying their hips as they walked and were teasing one another.

"Those are feminine ladies who will kick your ass!" shouted Juan over the music coming from everywhere.

"They'll slice off your balls with cold contempt if you cheat on them, but will also demurely hold your arm as you take them out for the evening. They demand honorable and masculine complements to their powerful femininity. Until the feminists understand those ladies they'll never articulate a well-rounded example of what a woman should be. The Hemingway man was never an obstacle to this. Their misunderstanding of what he was saying about men was and is."

When we reached La Curva, the place where the bulls often hit the wooden barricades as they are forced to turn right onto Estafeta and toward the arena, Juan paused and said, "Come, I'll show you something about women and the Hemingway man."

We began walking down winding side streets away from the heart of the ancient part of the city and passed a cathedral that Verva once called, "so ugly that no film would do it justice." The narrow streets grew emptier. The people's demeanor softened. Back in the heart of the festival, the women were mostly young and dressed like the men. As we moved away from the center of the city, the women were more often in dresses.

In a 1923 article in the *Toronto Star Weekly*, Hemingway wrote, "Really beautiful girls, gorgeous, bright shawls over their shoulders, dark, dark-eyed, black-lace mantillas over their hair, walk with their escorts in the crowds that pass from morning until night along the narrow walk that runs between inner and outer belts of café tables under the shade of the arcade out of the white glare of the Plaza de la Constitución."

Ladies don't wear fine dresses in the heart of this fiesta anymore. That isn't a recent change. Years after his novel helped to popularize and alter this fiesta, Hemingway wrote in *The Dangerous Summer*, "Pamplona is no place to bring your wife. The odds are all in favor of her getting ill, hurt, or wounded or at least jostled and wine squirted over her, or of losing her; maybe all three."

Ray Mouton, author of the book *Pamplona: Running the Bulls, Bars, and Barrios in Fiesta De San Pamplona*, would echo Hemingway that evening at the Windsor on the main plaza when he told me, "You don't bring a lady to Pamplona. Here she is going to get vomit on her dress. Here some drunken louse is going to fondle her. Here she won't sleep and will be pushed and jostled all over the festival. You can bring a girl and maybe a woman to Pamplona, but never a lady. So my wife stays in France."

Far away from the main square and from the sloppiest drunks and people pissing on walls, Juan began to show me smaller plazas and side streets where Spanish families were gathering at tables to have calm drinks and to play and hear Spanish guitar or folk music. We soon saw the Spanish ladies Hemingway first described with the bright shawls around their shoulders. There were children playing in the sun. All of them were in white and red and seemed unaffected by the madness and intoxicated rabble filling the city.

Such a juxtaposition of rabble to ladies is hard to find or even fathom in America. Americans fence off and hide partying adults in Vegas and behind walls at rock concerts and clubs. Yet in Spain they fit together as pieces of a society. Spain has its problems, but in Spain vice can still openly be refined into a virtue.

Juan said, after a lady in a white dress with a red shawl passed us, "God bless Spanish women. They're still Catholic enough to understand that wine and celebration aren't in opposition to morality, but when handled correctly are expressions of the same.

"Here when some drunk disparages a lady," said Juan, "the Spanish police show immediately with their batons and take the idiot away. The offender won't be back. They'll spend the rest of the fiesta in a Spanish jail. Here cops are moral figures, not lost in the red-tape of American legalism."

A group of Spanish families who were spread out on wooden picnic tables said "Hola" to us and offered us plastic cups of sangria. We accepted. It was lower-grade sangria that the Spanish call *kalimotxo*. It's just cola and red wine mixed in equal proportions and loaded with ice. In the cool shade out of the harsh mountain sun and with these open people, we drank and talked of the Hemingway man's love of a good drink but also his demand that a man doesn't become a fool with drink.

After thanking them again and moving on to the walls of the old part of the ancient city, we shifted our thoughts, if not our eyes, from the women to what Hemingway was showing us by sending his cast of characters in *The Sun Also Rises* on this pilgrimage to Pamplona.

Many critics have said Hemingway modeled Jake after himself. Hemingway and Jake do have similarities. They were both wounded in World War I. They both had worked as foreign correspondents. They both liked their drinks and the bullfights. They both hunted in Africa. They both loved Paris. So yes, Hemingway seems to have used himself for much of the Jake character. But thinking Jake is Hemingway is assuming too much. Hemingway took a man based loosely on himself who had a war wound that left him impotent and had him follow the steps he'd taken from Paris to Pamplona. Hemingway would later stress that Jake still had all his male parts and that his impotence wasn't psychological. He'd met wounded soldiers while in an Italian infirmary during World War I who'd had wool from their clothing driven into their scrotums by mortars or land mines. He wondered what it would be like for a man with all the usual hormones and feelings to be left physically— and therefore incurably—impotent even though he still had the plumbing. He then sent this character named Jake off on a pilgrimage with an assortment of Lost Generation types based on real people he'd known.

Lady Brett was based on Mary Duff Twysden, a woman Hemingway knew in Paris and went to Pamplona with. Her second marriage was to Sir Roger Thomas Twysden, a naval officer. Though she would divorce him, this gave her the title "Lady." Lady Duff died at only forty-five years old of tuberculosis. After her passing, Hemingway said with admiration, "Her pallbearers were all her ex-lovers." He also noted that Lady Duff ruined the real Robert Cohn character, a man named Harold Loeb. She had an affair with Loeb and, according to Hemingway, "The days with Lady Duff Twysden ruined poor Loeb for the rest of his life."

The comparison was so obvious that when *The Sun Also Rises* was published, Harold Loeb said he would kill Hemingway on sight. When Hemingway heard this, he said he sent Loeb a telegram telling him he'd be at Le Trou dans le Mur, a bar in Paris, for the next three evenings. "I chose this joint because it is all mirrors," Hemingway told A. E. Hotchner. "If you sit in the back you can see whoever comes in." Harold never showed. About a week later, Hemingway says he was eating at Brasserie Lipp when he spotted Harold Loeb. Hemingway says he went over and put his hand out to Harold and that Harold took his hand before realizing what he was doing and then yanked it away while saying, "Never."[1]

According to this account, by confronting Harold amicably but boldly, he squashed the threat. Though the account is one-sided, it is an example of how the Hemingway man is supposed to behave. The thing is, Hemingway told different versions of how he and Loeb got along after the novel was published. In a letter to Charles A. Fenton in 1952, Hemingway wrote: "The man [Harold Loeb] who identifies himself as Cohn in *The Sun Also Rises* said to me, 'But why did you make me cry all the time?' I said, 'Listen, if that is you then the narrator must be me. Do you think that I had my prick shot off or that if you and I had ever had a fight I would not have knocked the shit out of you? We boxed often enough so you know that. And I'll tell you a secret: you do cry an awful lot for a man.'"

Hemingway's propensity to inflate a story in one way or another, depending on his mood and audience, always makes his real-life story a deceptive thing.

As Juan walked that afternoon, the sun shined brightly over the yellow and white buildings and red-tiled rooftops. The din fell behind us as we walked but played on like background music from a perfect summer block party.

---

[1] A. E. Hotchner, *Papa Hemingway, a Personal Memoir*, Scribner's, 1955.

We stopped on a height at the edge of town and looked over the green countryside dotted with red-roofed villas and sliced by strips of green we knew were vineyards.

Juan pointed to corrals below. Black Spanish fighting bulls were standing solemnly in ancient pens, waiting to run the streets of Pamplona and to die in the Plaza de Toros. He sat on a stone step in the ruin of an ancient fort, let the sun bathe his face, and played with the gray goatee on his face as he thought about what to say. In the presence of all this death and celebration, he seemed like a yogi counting his *japa malas* beads.

I sat down beside him and let the moment be silent as cloud shadows moved across the rolling landscape and drums beat in the distant background.

After a few minutes, he said, "There are many ways to find your rite of passage to manhood. My way has been to run with the bulls."

Juan nodded his head toward a group of men and women, arms around one another, swaying, moving toward the center of the city and the party in their white-and-red outfits, and said, "A man needs to find through experience that in a crisis he can keep his head. That's what running has done for me. It teaches you what you can do. It takes away your fear. It allows you to confront and thereby control yourself even though you can't control forces, such as, in this case, fighting bulls. This builds courage to do what your head and heart together tell you to do even in the dramatic moments of your life."

Juan looked up at the ancient city and said, "Men are losing their way today because we no longer understand these tests. The rite of passage you're trying to understand is no longer understood, often no longer even allowed. Bullfighting and with it running might be gone soon, too. This is because this ancient rite of passage is no longer understood even by most of those who endure it."

He pointed back to people walking up a narrow street a hundred feet below us and said, "You can't tell by looking at someone whether or not they've learned to be a man, but when you run you'll see who understands and who isn't even trying. Many don't have a chance, as they don't know that running with the bulls lets you experience life by showing you a glimpse of death. Sure, many feel it. Grown men fall apart before the bulls even get to them in the street. But because they don't understand what they're doing or even know to try, they don't gain much from the experience."

He paused as his mind ran over the dilemma. Cloud shadows continued to move across the landscape as we sat listening to the city sing. He said, "Close to where we stood for the Chupinaza is where an American died in 1995. He was killed by a bull because he didn't understand how to run."

Juan was talking about Matthew Peter Tassio of Glen Ellyn, Illinois. Tassio made two fatal mistakes: When the bulls pounded close, he sprinted across the street, not with the crowd and the bulls, as you should; as a result, another runner knocked him down. He then broke the cardinal rule of running with the bulls: He got up in front of a bull. A Spanish fighting bull is a wild animal. It will destroy whatever moves in front of it. Its horns are sharp and curved forward. The lead bull drove a horn into Tassio's aorta and flung him across the street without even losing its place in front of the herd. Tassio got to his feet once more before falling dead.

"You must not make such mistakes."

Distant drums briefly pounded into an explosive rhythm sounding like a far-off thunderstorm. When the crescendo faded, Juan said, "This festival is a religious experience that begins with a statue of Saint Fermín you saw in the San Fermín Chapel. This is why Hemingway set his novel here. He wanted those members of the Lost Generation to find purchase on the old values. Jake had his Christian ideal and his name is Roland. After tomorrow's run we will go where Hemingway fished to understand this."

***

The next morning, after running with the bulls again and getting close but not close enough, we walked through the streets in early sun and clear mountain air to our rented van in an underground parking garage. During Hemingway's last San Fermín festival, he escaped with a small group on several days to picnic in the pine and beech wood mountains alongside streams and white villas with red tiled roves. He wrote in *The Dangerous Summer* that "we had found out how to beat the erosion of the fiesta and get away from the noise that was getting on the nerves of some of the more valued members of our group. It was to leave in the afternoon and drive up the Irati River above Aoiz and picnic and swim and then drive back in time for the bullfights. Each day we drove further up that lovely trout stream into the great virgin forest of the Irati that was unchanged since the time of the Druids. I had expected it would be all cut and destroyed but it was still the last great forest of the Middle Ages with its great beeches and its centuries-old carpet of moss that was softer and lovelier to lie on than anything in the world. . . . By the forest road we could make our way to nearly all the places we had to hike or pack into at the time I wrote about in *The Sun Also Rises* although you would still have to walk and climb from the Irati to Roncevalles."

We found, another half century later, that the forest and its big beech trees and moss so deep it felt like wet tundra under foot was still there. More than that, we found the Hemingway man's symbol was there.

In the novel, Hemingway's fictional group splits up and plans to regroup later in Pamplona for the fiesta. Insecure Robert Cohn waits for Lady Brett—who was off with another man. Robert was supposed to follow Jake but never did. He was too busy waiting on Brett with his juvenile heart in his pants.

Jake and Bill traveled up the Irati valley to Burguete in what is a peaceful escape to wilderness in the novel. Many have wondered why this interlude is in the novel. And why Burguete ("Burguete" is Castilian; the Basques call it "Auritz"), which is miles from the Irati River and other trout streams. Stoney says, "They go to Burguete because it's the closest village to the Roncevaux [the French spelling for the Spanish Roncevalles], which is in the pass Roland was ambushed and killed in."

Roncevaux is the pass in the Pyrenees where Charlemagne's rear guard, under command of Roland, was ambushed and destroyed on August 15, 1778. The history of this battle has been smothered in mythology. Various accounts say Saracens in league with local Basques ambushed Roland and his men as they fell behind Charlemagne, slowed by the weight of the booty taken from Pamplona. Other accounts say Basques, with their strong mountain legs, attacked Roland and his men in the steep mountain pass. Still other accounts say it was Spaniards resisting a Frankish invasion who ambushed Roland and his men. Whatever the facts, the most famous telling of the battle created its mythology. In the French epic *La Chanson de Roland* (*The Song of Roland*), written between AD 1040 and 1115, Roland is depicted as the ideal Christian knight. He is brave, chaste, loyal, and virtuous. But like the heroes of the Ancient World, he had a fatal flaw. When he was ambushed, he was slowed by pride and so blew his horn to summon help too late. By the time Charlemagne heard Roland's horn, Oliphant, and returned, all he saw were his enemies fleeing uphill with the goods taken from Pamplona on their backs. All he found in the pass was his demolished rear guard alongside Roland's body.

Along with his resounding horn, schoolchildren were once taught that Roland had a famous sword named Durendal. This mythology cast Roland as the ideal man. In the Middle Ages, Roland was what Odysseus was to the Ancient Greeks and what Aeneas was to the Ancient Romans. He was human and fallible but still too perfect to be real. He was a guiding light in the turbulent sea of human life, a compass bearing for boys and men.

Like other Christian knights of the Middle Ages, the mythical figure that became Roland was so chaste, loyal, and virtuous, we wouldn't find him realistic enough for a comic book hero today. He was a warrior who drew his strength from idealized Christian values. He was a warrior for God.

The divine was mingled within his knightly principles. It was these ideals and their icons that the evils of World War I's trench warfare and gas attacks cracked apart. The fissures in the foundation of these old ideals resulted in the so-called Lost Generation.

Hemingway, as a protestant from the American Midwest who'd moved to Paris to perfect his prose, had one foot in the old values and the other in the confusion of the new. In *The Sun Also Rises*, and many of his later works, Hemingway was trying to bridge the gap between the two with his code to create a new ideal. This was the divide I saw in Paris between the urban sophisticate and the manly hunter, soldier, and rural adventurer Hemingway also personified.

Of course, it's too simplistic to say World War I dashed the idealized Christian hero from popular appeal. Actually, our conception of heroism has always been in flux, and the Christian hero has been questioned since, to put a date on it, Cervantes published his first volume of *Don Quixote* in 1605.

Still, the shift from a hero who is chivalric, brave, and pious, and thinks he is fighting for right over wrong, to one who is flawed, dark, mysterious, and doesn't feign to know if he is really good or evil happened, for the most part, in the last few centuries. This is something Hemingway's heroes tried to make sense of, even as they lost. Hemingway knew and wrote about the deterioration of a man's strength and even moral virtues, but gave his strongest characters dignity even in their decline and fall. To Hemingway, keeping your dignity even in physical decline and death is a reflection of deep, manly virtues.

The leading man in Hemingway's novel *For Whom the Bell Tolls*, Robert Jordan, dies, but on his own terms. The hero of *The Old Man and the Sea,* Santiago, loses his great fish and is left broken and penniless, but still has his manly pride beneath his failing body. In *The Sun Also Rises,* the bullfighter Pedro Romero represents this ideal. Someday a bull will kill him or he'll lose his nerve or simply become too old to fight; nevertheless, as he goes he must, ideally at least, keep his dignity by retaining his bearing, his pride, his manly demeanor. That's a metaphor for how to live as a man.

This is why Hemingway placed Roland in the background of this novel's pilgrimage. Jake was a tragic figure looking to steady himself. Though Roland was simplistic, he was solid.

Gerald Brault's 1978 edition of *The Song of Roland*—published to commemorate the passage of 1,200 years since Roland's death—stresses in its commentary that this mythic epic about Roland shows how the Christian hero views life "as a series of difficult choices, the correct response requiring one to follow the hard road" and how its central "agnostic metaphor" envisions life as "a never-ending Roncevaux that must be faced with courage and with faith." This is the stoic and manly path Jake takes in the novel and that has often been misunderstood today—but that nevertheless, by its very aura, still draws legions of fans to Hemingway.

When Hemingway wrote *The Sun Also Rises,* the World War I generation likely still had verses from *The Song of Roland* in their schoolbook memories, as Hemingway did. Today's generations, however, know little about this idealized Christian knight. It's no coincidence that as mythical manly figures like Roland faded from popular understanding, society began to question increasingly why men were losing their way—and not knowing why.

This is why Juan took me and a few others to the pass where Roland died and rose up as a myth. Stoney said, "Hemingway thought his allusions to Roland would be obvious to readers, and they were to his generation, but today I've found that my students haven't heard of Roland. To students who ask why Hemingway didn't name Roland, I used to reply that it's impossible to say Roncevaux without thinking of Roland." Stoney says he learned his students didn't accept this answer. He had to educate his students on a topic that every primary schoolkid would have known a century ago.

Stoney says he was once leafing through *The Sun Also Rises* and "uttered the word 'Roncevaux'" while his grandmother was in the room. She said, *"Ah que ce cor a longue haleine."* (That horn has been blowing a long time.) Stoney was surprised. How did she know that line? She said she'd learned the old French version of that line from the *Song of Roland* as a girl. To her, it was a normal thing to know. Stoney says this taught him that "what may sometimes seem to be the submerged part of the iceberg is really the tidemark of the decline of cultural literacy." Stoney soon began helping his students learn about this classic piece of literature as they take college courses on Hemingway.

Hemingway clearly knew this history. He refers to Roland in letters and in the original manuscript of the posthumously published novel *The Garden of Eden*. In this novel, Hemingway's character, David Bourne, looks at mountains beyond Hendaye and thinks "beyond them would be Navarra and Navarra was Navarra. *Ah que ce cor ha longue haleine.*" (Another version of the line from *The Song of Roland*.) But an editor cut this French line from the novel, slicing away any reference to Roland. Because of this edit, Stoney says "readers are deprived of the recurrent and haunting presence of Roland in Hemingway's creative imagination, probably because the editor did not know what the quotation means, where it's from, and what it signifies—a kind of double whammy of cultural illiteracy."

It was interesting to hear this from Stoney, but altogether different to see this ground spreading before us just as Hemingway described it in the 1920s.

As Juan drove, we crossed a plateau beneath mountains decorated with green pine and beech trees and between hedged hay fields. We stopped at the Hotel Burguete in the small village of Burguete. The inn is white, three stories tall, and in the center of the village. The street wends between a church and shops before cutting through green and tan farm fields. We went into the inn for lunch and sat at a long hardwood table as the owner hurried over the creaky planks of the wood flooring to bring us wine and menus.

At the other end of the room was a piano Hemingway's first wife, Hadley, is said to have played. This has been disputed. The word "Hemingway" is carved under the lid of the piano (we looked), but earlier travelers noted that Hemingway was spelled wrong (the g had been left out). This has since been fixed. Also, the room Hemingway stayed in is upstairs, but even this is debated, as a floor was added to the inn years after Hemingway stayed there in the 1920s. Richard, one of our crew and a homebuilder by trade, pointed out that the room couldn't be the same one. They might have lifted the roof to add a floor, but they couldn't have lifted an entire floor, as well.

We shrugged. He stayed here and placed his characters here in *The Sun Also Rises* for a reason. It's this reason we were here to explore, not the precise facts about which room he stayed in or whether his first wife had played the piano.

In the novel, Jake and two others walk from this inn to fish the clear pools and stony riffles of the Irati River for trout. Stoney wanted to see if men could do this walk in the time Hemingway allotted. He showed up here with a hundred members of the Hemingway Society. They walked hard from this inn following the path Hemingway describes to the streams. They found there was no way Jake and his companions could have walked from the inn to fish the Irati in the time Hemingway said they did. They also found that the river where he set the fishing isn't even the Irati. They fished the Little Fabrica. Its ground is well described in the novel. Still, the Little Fabrica is too far to walk to in the time sequences he set in the novel. So why didn't Hemingway have them stay in the smaller village of Fabrica, which is along the sections of the streams fished? Why did he instead entirely omit the village of Fabrica (which means "factory" in Spanish) and the eroding walls of a factory still there today?

To explain this oddity with a writer who always paid close attention to real details, Stoney points to another site Hemingway had Jake and others visit while on their fishing excursion. They go just a few miles toward the mountains and France to visit the monastery at Roncesvalles, which is located at the Spanish foot of the pass where Roland was killed. This has long been an important point on the *Santiago de Compostela* pilgrimage route. There is a tombstone near the pass commemorating the area where it is traditionally held Roland succumbed to his wounds.

Founded in the eleventh century, the monastery at Roncevaux has always been of major importance to *El Camino de Santiago* (the way to St. James). A twelfth-century poem praises the monastery's hospitality: "The door lies open to all, to sick and strong; Not only to Catholics but to pagans, to Jews, heretics, idlers, vagabonds; In short, to good and bad, sacred and profane."[2]

Monastery records from as late as the seventeenth century say that as many as 25,000 meals were served to hungry pilgrims annually. The numbers of pilgrims passing through Roncesvalles now reaches as many 200,000 per year as people walk the way to the Apostle's tomb in Compostela. The monastery's church, which was rebuilt in 1400 after a fire, is considered to be one of the earliest examples of Gothic architecture in Spain. Just outside the walls of the monastery is a small Romanesque hermitage and a quadrangular crypt that marks the spot where Roland is said to have died. For medieval pilgrims, visiting the site where this Christian hero was slain was almost as important as the journey to Santiago.

After lunch in the inn, we drove to the monastery and visited its tombs and the Gothic chapel. As we walked in the sacred place and saw the tomb of Roland, we felt that this was Jake's, as the Hemingway man, time in the wilderness. Jake is contemplative and at peace with nature and himself here. Robert, by contrast, can't settle down within himself. He chases a woman who won't have him and can't

---

[2]www.pilgrimpathways.com/pilgrim_pathways.asp?IdSeccion=1&IdNoticia=30.

let her go. He is unmoored. If he'd come on this excursion and opened his mind, he might have found peace in the old values. Instead, Robert paces the streets of Pamplona waiting for Lady Brett to show and waiting to fight all her other suitors, like the juvenile ass he is.

Jake, in contrast, is moored by a code of values woven with the mythical figure of Roland. The myth of Roland is a connection to what we can't know. He is an ideal, though today we no longer trust iconic figures. We tear them down by pounding away at their flaws. We swarm when an actor or politician is caught in an affair or misdeed. They are not perfect nor is it possible to be perfect—a man like the mythologized Roland or Sir Gawain cannot exist in such a state of grace—so we say they can't even be guiding lights. Hemingway saw this and knew we need a new myth, a new ideal wed to a code but also to the reality that we all are tragic, that we all err and die, but nevertheless still can do beautiful things in the motion of a complicated life. This theme runs through *The Sun Also Rises* but also in much of what Hemingway wrote. It has often been said Hemingway was obsessed with the code. I was finding he was obsessed with a myth that can transform us by wedding us to the mysteries of a code of manly values.

I wondered about all this to Juan, and he nodded without saying much and then drove us up the mountain pass above Roncesvalles. We parked at the top in a grass clearing near rocks that were a vantage where we could see France to the north and Spain to the south, both descending into foothills of the forested Pyrenees and to green and tan fields in the hazy distance.

We walked south down a dirt path to where Juan worked out that James Michener had a magical picnic he described in his book *Iberia* with other writers and lovers of Spain. They picnicked in a place where seven rivulets come together under beech trees so old their branches were twisted and gnarly and some of their roots were above the ground in the forest below the road. They sat with their backs against the great trees on moss so thick "it seemed as if defeated knights had slept on it the night before." They talked about Pamplona and what brought them to its fiesta and how Hemingway's books had all been an important part of what took them there.

Juan brings a group of literate men and women to this place each fiesta. He waits for the right day, when the fiesta is roaring along and people are looking for a break from its endless madness. The weather also must be clear, as on all but the clearest days mist covers these mountains and flows like rivers down its passes. Michener wrote that the mist descended down the pass and over them like a stream of heavy clouds leaving them in a dream world where Roland's horn Oliphant might still echo.

There is no sign or marker showing where Michener took his group of authors and Pamplona aficionados. Juan found it by reading the text closely and studying the ground. You can find it, too. It's obvious when you see it and unchanged from when Michener was there more than a half-century ago. The moss might be deeper and the trees a few inches thicker, but if anything the magic of the place has increased.

If you happen there during the fiesta and see Juan and his group leaning their backs on the old beech trees by the seven rivulets telling stories and reading passages from Hemingway and Michener, walk quietly in and sit down and become a part of the scene. You'd be welcome. If you do, you'll see something like Brigadoon, that legendary town in Scotland that appears for just one day every hundred years to weary travelers. It's a magical thing that, like the true basis of a man, can be sent away as fast as a mirage by a loud tone and unseeing eyes.

STEP 4

The Gauntlets

When heaven is about to confer a great responsibility on any man,
it will exercise his mind with suffering, subject his sinews and
bones to hard work, expose his body to hunger, put him to poverty,
place obstacles in the paths of his deeds, so as to stimulate his
mind, harden his nature, and improve wherever he is competent.

—Mencius

SOMETIMES YOU FORGET YOU ARE mortal. This is
not a good thing. This is a stupid thing.

I stood in a deep shadow at the head of the canyon of shut-
tered bars that is Estafeta during a bull run. No one stands at
the head of Estafeta and just around "La Curva" unless they
are very stupid or very skilled. I thought I was skilled enough.
I was wrong. At La Curva there are heavy wood barricades to

force the bulls to turn right down Estafeta, the longest and most crowded portion of the run toward the arena.

The only other men waiting with me were a few Basques and a very naive Aussie. The Basques stood set like sprinters. One little Basque was getting solemn and respectful nods from runners who knew the field as they walked by this spot to take places in the packed street farther up Estafeta.

We heard the first rocket explode. The bulls were coming. It seemed like forever this time. Many people were running frightened past us and up Estafeta. As they did, all the runners were looking back toward where the bulls would come with melting expressions. These first people I knew were the *valientes*. I checked the Basques. Many people were running frightened past us and up Estafeta.

I could see another American, an experienced runner on his tenth Pamplona, on the other side of La Curva. I'd met him at a bar the day before with other foreign runners. This runner stands on the left just before La Curva. He lets the bulls pass him. The bulls will typically be on the right side of the street before they hit La Curva and follow the left side until the crowd pushes them back to the middle. His technique is to get between the bulls when a bull falls or slips at the 90-degree turn. He'll then run the horns until he must dodge away. I wasn't ready for that approach, but he advised me—if I got my timing right—that I could stand just around La Curva and run before I could see the bulls. He said to run when "the people's eyes are trying to see through the backs of their heads."

My timing was wrong. I didn't see when the Basques ran. They were just gone, ahead of the bulls. A runner came around La Curva looking at me wildly in the eyes and screaming, "Run. Run."

I ran, but it was too late.

I turned my head and saw the bulls hitting the barricades without a pause. The old guidebooks said this might give a little time. There are holes in the plywood where bull horns have punched through. But the officials now put something on the ground to keep the bulls from slipping and falling, as they too often fell on runners—dead foreigners make for bad tourism. So the bulls took the turn too fast for me to have a chance.

I was sprinting. The bulls were going maybe twenty-five miles per hour. The crowded street down the long bending straightway before the curve into the arena would slow them. The Basque runners knew this. It was why they ran when they did. They wanted to be in front of the horns when the bulls slowed just enough to have a glorious run right in front of the forward-facing horns of the Spanish fighting bulls.

The bulls were still bunched up in a stampede and were almost on top of me.

I dodged right to get out of their way but bumped into people, who knows how many, trying to do the same thing. I was ping-ponged back out in front of the horns. I saw a hole and went left to where I knew I shouldn't be—but the rules are made to be broken when you sense an opening. I was going on instinct. It's the last of the help you get.

I made the wall of an ancient home. I flattened into it. No one understands how flat the human body can become until you must pancake into a wall to avoid the bulls. A 2,000-pound white steer with his horns curved down like a snowplow was leading the tight group of steers and bulls. The lead steer's head was swinging side to side with his swaggering gait as he ran fast—too fast to run in front of.

The huge steer passed me and plowed down runners beyond me. The six black fighting bulls were in a bunch behind the white steer with the snowplow horns. The first passed me clean. One behind was running along the wall. This bull saw me. He turned his sharp horns to spear me. I turned my body just enough and he missed. I don't know how. He hooked an Aussie next to me and sent him sprawling. Maybe the bull wanted him all along.

The bulls disappeared into the moving crowd of runners, and all those clinging to the sides like spiders let go and began to breathe again.

I took a deep breath. The close call was marvelous. The chance of being gored makes this real. Even the great runners have been gored. Legends like Matt Carney, David Rodriguez, Julen Madina, and Juan Pedro Lecuona were gored and all ran again. There have been about fifteen fatalities during the run in the last century, but there are usually about a dozen gorings a year. I didn't mind the near miss. What bothered me was being caught so foolishly.

An American named Larry who has a white beard and a back slouched from his years, a man I'd met at the Chapel San Fermín, popped out of a heavy wood door from one of the apartment buildings along the street. He saw me. He is an old amigo of Juan's who moved to Pamplona because the place is in his soul.

"You shouldn't be here," he said, looking me over with caring eyes. "This is the worst place to be. The bulls always hug this wall."

I nodded. He was right. I'd run all wrong. It nearly cost me. That night I got very drunk.

***

That afternoon, in dappled afternoon sunlight filtering through green leaves on old beech trees in a small Pamplona park, I met a former US Army soldier who deepened my view of this mistake. About fifty people were drinking cheap red wine from plastic cups. They were of every age and were mixing in the currents of the fiesta. Some had come with another generation and now came themselves. Many were women. Most were native English speakers. This was one of the little gatherings foreign runners hold daily during the fiesta.

I started talking to a tall man with thin lips and gray temples. His name is John Schumacher. He is a corporate executive who works in one of those high-rises in downtown Manhattan, but before his first Pamplona he had fought in Vietnam. He had been a door gunner. His job in the war was to protect soldiers as they were dropped off and picked up in hot landing zones in those humid jungle clearings.

Birds were singing in the branches above us. I noticed this because it was the first time in days when the background din of voices and music was low enough to hear something as soft as birdsong. I looked from the birds to John and asked why he runs.

He shrugged as he said, "Running is grand. It keeps me in touch with life, real honest life."

He paused as he looked up at the birds hopping branch to branch. He then rolled his head around his shoulders. As he is a tall, lean man, I was looking up at him. At times like this, I like to give people the silence to find their words.

He finally said, "When people ask me about the war with those little smiles on their faces and naivety in their eyes— and I know you haven't asked," he said as he nodded and his expression showed he was looking back, "when someone asks about that I ask them to tell me about their mother's death or their father's or whomever close they've lost, as that is how personal what they're asking me is."

John smiled and shifted his head with his thoughts as we stood in that little park. He said, "What I'm getting to is that in Nam many died before they could learn how they might spot a tripwire. Others died because they lost their heads and did crazy things that were heroic but also head- less. But in war, as in running with bulls, you're never safe and never in control. What both can teach you is the only thing you can control is how you take it. Can you control your fear, your excitement? Can you learn and do the smart things in those mad moments? That's why I run. It keeps me humble, keeps me remembering that."

He flashed a wry smile. John's hair is graying, but his tone is young. He has the American executive's bearing and a lot of charm. He was wearing a faded short-sleeve polo shirt and jeans. He said, "A few years ago I stood in the street next to this young couple from the states. She clearly didn't want to be there and didn't belong. She had no idea what to do. I could tell her fiancé didn't know either and that he was going to try to protect her—you can't do that with the bulls. It will only get you hurt, maybe really hurt. So I said to her, 'Excuse me, I think you should know that a young American woman who was standing just about where we are got stepped on by a bull last year. The bull stepped on her head. I saw some of the fluid from her skull run onto the street. They took her away in a stretcher. She lived, but she'll never get out of bed again.' That woman left the street and a bunch of people thanked me. She didn't need to be there. No one does, I guess. But if you're going to run you should at least open your eyes to what's happening."

I nodded as I said, "It's fun, but it's not a game."

"Yes, exactly," said John. "This isn't a fake thing." Then his tone shifted to contemplation: "You know, I came to Pamplona the first time because I didn't want to go back to the world after Vietnam. I was chasing girls around Europe to forget about the war. When I got here I found this incredible group of people who'd found this ritual, this getting into the street with bulls, to keep themselves grounded. These people keep me coming back. I thought I was searching for a diversion, but I was really trying to understand, to come to terms with what's real."

He then repeated a line that is a favorite of this group: "Running with the bulls is cheaper than therapy."

I asked if he'd ever been hurt and John pointed to a scar beside his left eye. "A bull got me here a few years ago. I'd been arrogant. I felt immortal the way some young soldiers do. I took one step too many in front of the horns. I knew I should have dodged out of their way, but I tried to stay in front just like Matt Carney once did. I was knocked unconscious and was in critical condition." He shrugged, laughed at what a dumb thing that was. I almost blushed as my mistake repeated in my head.

John's perspective clarified my thoughts. I'd become too at ease with the bulls. Such lessons are a part of the gauntlet.

Arrogance will come, and you have to recognize it not as a friend but as a tool to be understood and used. At the other extreme, fear is a helpful thing unless it controls you. If it takes control it can get you killed. Such is the line a man must walk. I'd regained my fear that day without payment in blood. I would do better the next morning.

I admit that this is what the gauntlet is about. The gauntlet is the longest and hardest part of a rite of passage. G. Gordon Liddy popularized the method of attaining manliness by facing your fears in his autobiography, *Will*. I once had the opportunity to ask Liddy about how he faces his fears after he kindly had me on his radio show in 2008. He said, "I thought I had invented facing fear to grow as a man, but later I found that psychologists call it the 'process of desensitization.' It doesn't work immediately, but each time you face a fear the fear diminishes. It also isn't something you only have to do once. A man will have to confront his weaknesses throughout his life to grow as a man, a potential hero.

"When I was a boy I learned to face my fears to overcome them and achieve anything; for example, when I was eight there were these freighters along the New Jersey shore that frightened me, so I worked up the courage and slipped by security guards and climbed the monstrous things. I was detected and chased, but got away. Afterward I was proud of myself. I was like a boy who'd faced a dark night and realized he was strong enough inside to overcome such things.

"It never ends though. You have to face your fears all your life. When I first went to prison I knew I'd better stand up and fight at the first opportunity, despite the odds of getting seriously hurt. So I did. I wound up in the hospital along with the inmate I fought, but it was worth it. My fear dissipated and one of the older convicts, a gang leader, said to me, 'Well, we found out your heart don't pump no Kool-Aid.'

"I'm seventy-eight years old now and there are a whole new set of things I have to face, as we all do as men," said Liddy. "Certainly, men need to use good judgment when facing their fears, but to be heroes they must continually master themselves. This is why I still think men should join the armed forces. The military will teach you that it's not all about you; that we're in something together. A man needs to learn selflessness or he'll just become selfish, and there's nothing manly or heroic about selfishness."

Liddy and Hemingway would have gotten along.

✳✳✳

Before the run the next morning, I entered the street at 7:00 a.m. and walked past the ornate city hall and went downhill on Santo Domingo to where the street deepens along a retaining wall. The street was wet from a street cleaner's brushes and smelled like a basement recently flooded. People were gathering in groups. Some were drunk. One of them was singing a Beatles song—"Hey Jude."

I walked by them smiling with them in the early sun. It was a lovely fresh morning for another run—one of eight in a row.

There is a man who sits on a stool and sells newspapers along Santo Domingo. He clears out before the bulls come. It's traditional for a runner to run with a rolled newspaper in his hand. The local newspaper *Diario de Navarra* is the traditional paper to buy and carry on the run. I bought a copy and kept walking downhill on the street to watch a procession place a statue of San Fermín in the recess of a wall and sing a song asking for the saint to protect the runners.

This is the beginning of the course. This section is a canyon between an old hospital and a cathedral. There is no place to hide here, and the bulls are running too fast to outrun. A man could bound across this section of street in three or four strides. At the bottom is the "suicide run." This is where some run at the bulls for a few strides before turning up the street and dodging the bulls. This is where Juan now runs, as the run is short and the chances are good you'll come through all right if you know what you're doing. This is no place for beginners.

I didn't go down this street to find a position to run. There is a little shop just down a side street where some veteran runners gather before the run. They buy newspapers and coffee and talk for a half hour before going up the street to their chosen positions.

On the way out, some stop to say a little prayer at that statue of San Fermín. They pray for the bulls, for a safe run, and for whatever is in their hearts.

I prayed for better judgment. I had been humbled and knew humbling a man is what the gauntlets are for. I leaned against the wall under the statue with my eyes closed and laughed at myself. Someone was saying something to me, but I didn't listen. My mind was raging. I felt how close I came not by chance but by arrogance, and it was eating at me. I thought how in this rite of passage one time through is frightening. It's a lively and foolish dare. It's skydiving once to say you did it. But if this were all there were to these manly trials, boot camp would be one day long.

The gauntlet is the largest portion of any true rite of passage. It is the marathon—the three months in boot camp, the weeks of football practice before the games begin, the being pummeled by a karate master in a dojo as you work for the belt, and then the next. It's a learning process and a struggle for your will to submit as you endure. You only get this out of it if you think and learn as the gauntlet breaks you down. Sometimes this means you must be hit. Other times you must play the fool. I think being the fool is worse. But there are those who don't care if they're the fool. These types must be treated like a bird dog that just doesn't care if you scold it but only learns not to chase deer from the shock of an electric collar.

I'm being too intense, I thought. Sure, to get the most out of such things we must think, but not too much. I recalled what Matt Carney said about running with bulls.

Carney is a legend to foreign *aficionados* of the San Fermín festival. In the mid-1960s, James Michener (1907–1997) wrote that Carney "spoke like a drunken angel." Carney was from California. He came to Europe to finish a novel. When in Paris, he was spotted by an agent looking for male models. Michener said Carney "had the rugged New World look of a Mississippi gambler, and French advertisers flocked to him in such numbers that he earned a great deal of money."[1] Carney bought homes all over Europe and lived a lavish lifestyle, but it was in Pamplona where he showed what he was made of. Each morning, Carney always seemed to be right in front of the horns as he ran up Estafeta with a mad grin on his pinup face.

---

[1]James Michener, *Iberia*, Random House, New York, 1968.

Michener asked Carney if running is "something mystical?"

Carney looked at Michener like he thought Michener was a madman.

They were in the main square in Pamplona during the festival. Carney had a black eye from that morning's run. He'd been on the horns again. A photo of Carney inches in front of the bulls had been on the front page of the morning newspaper. In the photo, Carney was "alone and laughing his Irish head off."

As Carney answered Michener, a crowd was listening: "Christ, you miss the whole flaming point," said Carney. "It's fun! It's joy! I run the bulls for joy, which is the chief ingredient of generosity. In this way I prove that I have the capacity to give myself whole hog to some activity."

"Do you run to prove your bravery?" pushed Michener.

Carney said, "To stand in the street before the run begins . . . to visualize the bulls coming at you . . . to sense what might happen . . . yes, that takes courage. But when those rockets go off and the black shapes come tumbling at you . . . hell, you've already made your commitment and all it takes now is a sense of joy . . . to be a part of the stampede."

Carney's words drummed joyously in my head as I walked with amigos up beyond La Curva to a position on Estafeta for the run. The street is a canyon with building walls clustered with balconies that were then jammed with people dressed in white and red, waiting to witness the madness of the run.

When I'd first read Carney's answer—years before I'd first run in 2007—I thought he viewed the run as a mad moment, not unlike train dodging or games of chicken. This was in keeping with how I'd first thought Hemingway treated the running with bulls in *The Sun Also Rises*. But now I know this becoming "part of the stampede" to prove you have "the capacity to give [yourself] whole hog to some activity" fits with the gauntlet of any rite of passage. We must understand, even soberly contemplate, but we also must become a joyous part of the moment. We must drop all that analytical reasoning and simply become a part of the stampede.

Professor Allen Josephs, who teaches literature at the University of West Florida in Pensacola and is the author of *On Hemingway and Spain*, was asked, "Was Hemingway actually courageous, or was he working out questions of courage and masculinity in his life and writing?"

Josephs said, "I don't know what the difference is. He was clearly courageous but courage comes at a high price and that price is part of any courage beyond the spontaneous act. Everybody is afraid. That's why we run with the bulls. Not that I run anymore and I was never good at it. The non-cowards got eaten by the saber-tooths and their genes dried up. The trick is all about how you work it out. So courage and working out questions of courage become the same thing and I think Hemingway was acutely aware of that convergence. And it's not a gender thing. Who is braver than Pilar [in *For Whom the Bell Tolls*]?"[2]

With these answers in mind, I stopped halfway up Estafeta. The street was crowded with anxious people. I thought how running with the bulls is really a silly thing. But so are climbing Everest, jumping from a plane for the thrill, heli-skiing, and BASE jumping. So is any serious risk

---

[2]www.thehemingwayproject.com/category/allen-josephs/.

taken for no obvious reason. The thing is, we no longer have to risk our lives to earn our sustenance—at least most of us. Most dangers can be avoided within the safety of our civilizations. So we must do real things to learn about ourselves and to build ourselves into who we wish to be.

So I smiled and looked at my feet in the pushing crowd. Surely life lived safely behind Sheetrock walls and in front of a thumping, flat-screen television is too false and sterile to take very seriously. Such a life doesn't make boys into men. To build character, we have to push ourselves, to test ourselves, even to take reasonable, if sometimes silly, risks. If we enjoy the challenges, even the hazards, all the better.

Like Hemingway's character Francis Macomber and the PH telling him to understand but not to talk about what it takes to make a man too much, I was overthinking, so I instead just let myself fall into the crowd.

When the bulls came, I ran for sheer joy. I didn't get close enough—feet, not inches—and then they were gone and I fell out of the stampede and all I wanted to do was try again.

STEP 5

The Codes

This above all: to thine own self be true, And it must follow, as the night the day, Thou canst not then be false to any man.

—Shakespeare, *Hamlet*, Act I, Scene III

SOMETHING HAPPENED IN THE BULLFIGHTING arena in pamplona that I'm told is quite common but that both shocked and impressed me.

The bulls, and the steers that run to lead them, had run through the sand in the arena. They'd been herded out by the *pastores*, men who wait with long sticks they swing with fast, jabbing movements meant not to give the bulls a moment to think. The *dobladores*, these are people with good bull-fighting knowledge (sometimes ex-bullfighters) who take up positions in the bullring with capes to coax the bulls toward the corral as quickly as possible, were folding their capes and gathering together with smiles on their faces and relief in their movements.

The runners were still flooding in. They pushed in with exuberant strides for several minutes until the sweepers—a group of steers sent along the course minutes after the bulls to pick up any bulls that have been separated from the herd—ran through. When the last of the steers were safely gone, the front gate to the Plaza de Toros was closed, trapping the runners who ran all the way into the arena. All around in the circular bullfighting arena, there looked to be a capacity crowd of 19,720 people waiting for mayhem to be set loose.

With the suddenness of a chute clanging open at a rodeo, a gate opened, and at full gallop a cow with leather covering her horns bolted into the arena. The crowd of runners split like a flock of blackbirds dodging a hawk. A few weren't spry enough. At full charge, the cow scooped up a man and sent him up into the air. Then another. The arena roared with the throaty cheers of all the spectators.

Okay, this wasn't a real Spanish fighting bull. These are what the Spanish call *vaquillas*. These are actually cows. They are mature and experienced cattle that have learned how to throw people with their leather-covered horns. The fighting bulls are never allowed to learn how to aim at men instead of moving capes. Fighting bulls would kill a lot more matadors if they knew how to fight men like this. But the *vaquillas* know.

After five or ten minutes, the *vaquilla* tires and slows, and the officials send a 2,000-pound ox into the arena to herd the smaller cow out of the limelight. The runners step back, awed by the sheer size of the mature bull that had been castrated before it reached maturity and so doesn't have a bull's intoxicating dose of testosterone.

Another *vaquilla* was then sent charging into the sand of the arena. People who have been caught near the gate with their attention elsewhere have been seriously injured, even killed, by a *vaquilla* on its first charge into the arena. The *vaquillas* come in at full gallop, as if they can't wait to pummel the runners waiting to play with them. But mostly the *vaquillas* only bruise and perhaps break a few ribs of the runners.

Though Hemingway likely didn't run with the bulls, he did get in and play with the *vaquillas*. He called this event "the amateurs." In his day, some would use shirts and coats as improvised capes to attempt passes with the *vaquillas*. No one tries that anymore—likely because the *vaquillas* used today are just too experienced. They are taken from town to town all summer in Spain. Playing with the *vaquillas* is a rite of passage all in itself. Hemingway boasts that he became a crowd favorite at the amateurs, as he and his group were the only people in the arena who weren't Spanish or Basque at the time. Hemingway used improvised "capes" to attempt passes with the cows and was beaten up by the *vaquillas* a few times, as was Harold Loeb (the inspiration for the Robert Cohn character in *The Sun Also Rises*). Loeb made the newspapers one day. A *vaquilla* picked him up on its horns and he went for a ride, holding the horns with his chest on the cow's face, until the cow suddenly stopped and Loeb went flying off but somehow landed on his feet and stayed upright. The crowd went wild. It looked like he'd done that on purpose.

The first time I watched this from a seat in the arena, what shocked and impressed me was that when the second *vaquilla* began to tire, a man with a ponytail and these brown shorts when everyone was wearing white grabbed its tail and was pulled along by the tired animal through the hundreds of runners in the arena. He was finally shaken off and started to swagger with this big grin splitting his tanned face. A right hook sent his glee slamming into the dirt of the arena. A Spaniard had leapt in the air and punched him square in the jaw. The man with the ponytail got up and staggered around. Two other Spaniards pummeled him back to the ground. I leaned forward, aghast. The entire arena was cheering as young Spanish or Basque men beat the man until he lay bloody and helpless in a fetal position.

This would happen three more times to other foreigners who didn't know the rules for playing with the *vaquillas*. These animals must be respected. Not respecting them properly means being disciplined by the ones who know the rules. Sometimes guides can be harsh.

The proper behavior for dealing with the bulls in the *encierro* (the running of the bulls) is announced on loudspeakers, can be read on printed notices, and there is a section on the official website (www.sanfermin.com) that explains the proper behavior for how to treat the bulls and the *vaquillas*. Sanfermin.com is a Spanish website, but there is an English version; in this section it says, "Be careful and try to follow a very simple rule: don't touch the animals and don't try to attract their attention, it is forbidden, as well as to take their tails or try to shake them. It could be dangerous, not only for you but also for the rest of the runners. . . . Keep your hands off the animals. Even the heifers who are in the bullring to be played with, should not be physically touched. The crowd turns on the culprits with a vengeance when this happens."

After the man with the ponytail had his ass thoroughly kicked, I turned and asked Juan if this was normal. "Yes," he said as the crowd roared and another *vaquilla* charged into the arena sending runners flying up and then back down onto the sand in the arena. "I have witnessed some severe beatings. Some do not know the rules or, in their enthusiasm, forget the rules and try to bulldog the *vaquillas*."

Many of those people who come on Hemingway's coattails just don't know about the rules of conduct, but the enforcement of this code isn't new. Hemingway witnessed this in 1923. He wrote, "A man who grabbed the bull by the tail was hissed and booed by the crowd and the next time he tried it was knocked down by another man in the bull ring."[1]

After the *vaquillas* were done, Juan and I walked down into the arena. Runners were standing in circles laughing and talking about how they fared. We stopped at the entrance to the arena and Juan said, "I'm not the lynch mob type, but one time I ran into the bullring after the bulls when one bull broke its leg and fell in the sand right here. A long-haired, shirtless asshole (I have the video somewhere) jumped on the fallen bull's kidneys and raised his arms in victory. While I was making a move to get to him and kick his ass, a sudden surge of around 20 *mozos* surrounded and beat the crap out him. He was carried to the *enfermeria*. Disrespect for the bulls is instantly punished."

---

[1]Ernest Hemingway, "Pamplona in July," the *Toronto Star Weekly*, October 27, 1923.

So the Spanish and the Basques in the arena enforce a code. They do this in a way Americans would never accept, in a way attorneys would sue out of existence in the US. This code requires that people respect the bulls and the *vaquillas*. By respecting them they are respecting themselves and the others with them.

This made it impossible for me not to run into the arena for a chance to be plowed by a *vaquilla*; after all, running with the bulls into the Plaza de Toros and then staying for the six *vaquillas* is as close as we can get today to finding ourselves in the Roman Coliseum.

I ran with the moving crowd and the bulls where the street turns and tightens as it goes into the arena. This is one of the most dangerous sections of the course. This is the place where Hemingway chose to have a man killed by a bull in *The Sun Also Rises*. Running down this tightening entrance with people scrambling, stumbling, pushing, and the bulls just ahead and behind felt a lot like a dog might on a busy freeway. Someone tripped on someone's feet and fell in front of me. I started to leap over him, but he popped up, nearly taking me down. Right behind me was a *suelto* (a lone bull) that had already gored several people on the course. I shoved this runner aside by driving my shoulders through him and sprinted forward with my eyes on the churning feet in front of me. The bull behind me had slowed to the pace of the runners, but falling in front of him might mean being horned or stepped on by the 1,200-pound animal.

I dashed into the arena and turned right to let the bull go past and to let the *pastores* clear the last bulls from the arena. One moment you're in shadow and on the horns just trying not to fall down and the next you're in bright sunlight in a circular arena surrounded by tens of thousands of screaming people. All around was the view a gladiator would have had in an amphitheater. Death is there in the dirt under your feet. Danger is there with you. How you act under this pressure matters to your well-being, and later to your view of yourself.

Staying for the *vaquillas* is a real, old-fashioned gauntlet. It's a coming-of-age ritual for young men all over Spain, as this isn't unique to Pamplona. Playing with *vaquillas* is a part of many fiestas. You can escape from Pamplona's arena by going over a wooden fence that separates the arena from the stands, but to do so you must fight through people lined up to watch people get pummeled.

The first *vaquilla* had to leap over a pile of *mozos* who test their manhood by lying face-forward at the place where the *vaquilla* runs in. A photographer who happened to have the apartment next to mine snapped a shot that made all the papers the next day. The photograph shows *vaquilla* leaping with its front legs tucked in as it cleared the men like a horse over a fence. The cow didn't land on anyone but quickly scooped someone up into the air and let him fall before going after others.

Time, you might suspect, should pass slowly in the arena when you're in with a cow that's adept at tossing people, but it actually flies by as you live in the moment. If you let your mind wander to the white face of the clock hanging at one end of the arena, you'd risk being caught by the constantly circling cow that has spent years learning to throw people. So I stayed in the moment and I had close escapes but wasn't thrown. I tried but missed on several attempts to touch the

Spanish newspaper in my hand to the *vaquilla's* rump. Doing that is considered an act of bravery—so there is something left for the next time.

After playing with the six *vaquillas,* I met Juan's groups of experienced runners for an amaretto and brandy at Txoko's up on the Plaza del Castillo.

"You played with the *vaquillas!*" said Curly, an American with curly white hair who has been coming to the fiesta for decades. He knocked his glass into mine and said, "We don't play with them until the last few days of the fiesta. They'll hurt you. They've caved in my ribs. When you're hurt like that you can't run the bulls anymore, so we wait."

I raised my glass to his practicality and asked about the rules for playing with the *vaquillas.*

"The *mozos* will still beat the crap out of anyone who dogs the *vaquillas,*" said Curly, "but over the years I've noticed they do less and less of that. The enforcement seems to be fading away. A shame. If it goes away completely the whole thing will fall apart. It'd become a steer-wrestling contest, not a game of respect and courage."

✳✳✳

I was impressed that rules for running with the bulls and playing with the *vaquillas* form a code of conduct that leads to a code of honor. When you respect the bulls, you also respect those around you—if you don't respect the bulls and so grab a bull's tail or do something else to make a bull turn around in the street, the bull will become what the Spanish call a *suelto* (a lone bull), and *sueltos* gore people. Bulls are much more docile when they are in the herd following or running with the steers. When they find themselves alone, they see the people around them as threats. The gorings played on TV each year are almost always done by a *suelto.* By respecting the bulls, and therefore those around you, you adhere to the idea that there is a universal code of values that you are a part of. You follow a code that demands that the bulls and the people deserve your respect.

This is the beginning of accepting a code of honor within yourself. In contrast, this is also why criminal gangs and even frats that have one code for themselves and another for everyone else don't form rites of passage that improve people. To be real, any rite of passage must help participants realize that everyone else has the same inherent rights as they do and that people should only be defined by their character—by the rules in a code. This is why the second rule in the Samurai's Code of Bushido, which translates to the "way of the warrior," is *Jin* (Benevolence): a magnanimous and compassionate state of mind that embraces the idea that all people are fundamentally the same and should be treated with the same respect regardless of station or situation.

In *The Sun Also Rises,* this manly code is never defined as it might be in a nonfiction book, but it is shown. When Robert Cohn had been dumped and thoroughly emasculated in Pamplona by Lady Brett, he begins to lash out as a child might. Robert, we are told in the first paragraph of the novel, "was once a middleweight boxing champion at Princeton." Jake, the narrator of the novel, says he is not very impressed with this boxing title, but that "it meant a lot to Cohn. He cared nothing for boxing, in fact he disliked it, but he learned it painfully and thoroughly to counteract the feeling of inferiority and shyness he had. . . ." Cohn didn't try to learn the manly code he was exposed to; he instead dealt with his juvenile insecurity by acting as a schoolyard bully who he didn't get his way.

He punches out Jake. He slugs a lot of people. When he finds the bullfighter, Pedro Romero, in a hotel room with Lady Brett, Cohn knocks him down again and again, but the bullfighter keeps getting back up. Romero doesn't have a chance, but he has so much pride, he won't stop getting up. This happens fifteen times. Finally, Cohn says he won't hit the bullfighter anymore. He says he just can't do it. Cohn had run into a man who'd earned his courage with bulls. When Cohn tells the bullfighter he'd be "ashamed" to hit him again, the bullfighter hits Cohn "as hard as he could in the face."

Romero then sits on the floor, his body beaten and exhausted, and Cohn tries to help the bullfighter back to a bed. The bullfighter, still full of manly pride, tells Cohn he'll kill him if he tries to help him up and he'll kill him either way if he doesn't get out of town.

When Cohn, still not sure what to do, tries to shake the bullfighter's hand, no hard feelings you know, the bullfighter hits him again. Cohn is baffled. He doesn't know why this bullfighter won't tacitly agree that his behavior is acceptable as long as they shake hands. Cohn seems stuck in some boyhood code. He never became a man. He doesn't know that to a man, a man like a bullfighter, there are real consequences for actions. By not shaking Cohn's hand, and thereby excusing Cohn's actions, Romero forces Cohn to dwell on what he'd done, possibly even to learn from his mistake.

Cohn leaves the room crying. He'd run into a man he couldn't beat with his fists. He'd run into something deeper than flesh, into a code of values.

Cohn feels embarrassed and he keeps crying; he doesn't know how to make sense of why everyone detests him or why he even loathes himself for acting this way.

Later Mike, one of the other characters on the pilgrimage, tells Jake he thinks the bullfighter "ruined Cohn. You know I don't think Cohn will ever want to knock people about again."

Many go through this metamorphosis in grade school. Cohn didn't run into the subtleties of this manly code until his middle thirties. Maybe it was too late for him. Cohn couldn't get over himself enough to comprehend that courage and skill are only tools of manliness. Having the balls to fight, after all, is hardly a definition of manliness; it's only a necessary ingredient. Knowing that action must be right before it is taken is manly. When it comes to hitting people, this basically means a man is restricted to self-defense or the defense of others when there is no other way out. Cohn never looks around to attempt to understand this or the universal code of values Jake was trying to show him. He doesn't see that learning to live with fear, learning to lead through fear, learning to be in control of yourself despite the fact you're not in control of anything else are some of the first steps to submitting to a code of honor. What Lady Brett had done to him gave him a chance to overcome adversity in a manly way, but he failed to understand that.

If he'd grasped this, he could have found that next comes learning to submit to what's right, to what must be done because it is right, while also learning never to submit to what's arrogant, foolish, unmanly—in sum, against the code—as are all necessary and hard-to-define parts of the code Hemingway alludes to, and that real rites of passage teach those who have their minds open.

If you're wondering why American sports stars, despite undergoing intense rites of passage, can at times behave so poorly, the reason is the code within their rite of passage has at times grown weak. Sports stars have become so revered and important to their franchises they're often coddled on college campuses and by professional teams and so don't always have to pay for bad behavior. If you don't pay for bad behavior, as Cohn did, you don't have a chance of growing from the experience. In contrast, a man or woman undergoing the trials of a military's boot camp are forced to pay for their mistakes.

This is part of the reason military personnel are so often manlier than sports stars. The more fundamental reason is that the members of today's US military are volunteers; they're volunteering to serve us, to protect us at home and abroad. This is a selfless adherence to a code of values that goes beyond themselves. Sure, many join the military for adventure, for the college money, to prove themselves, and for other egocentric reasons; nevertheless, they have agreed to fight and possibly die for us and our way of life, and on some level they know this. To nail this down into something comprehensible, each branch of the armed services has a well-defined code of honor. (You can find many of them in the back of this book.)

If Robert Cohn had made these leaps, if he could have gotten over himself just a little bit, he might have found that a real code of honor actually takes weight off your shoulders and puts it on the greater thing you're living for. He would have found it much easier to set mistakes and troubles aside if he had understood the code Jake was trying to show him, as a code gives a person the chance to define a wrong or weakness of character clearly and then to get past those things. All you have to say is, well, that was a mistake, but now I'm doing the right thing so that isn't me anymore, and it is behind you; instead, Cohn placed the entire burden of his mistakes on his self-identity, which was a very superficial and unstable thing to set such weighty faults on.

Of course, misunderstanding the rules of a code is very common. This happens to everyone at some point on any real rite of passage. Some, like Cohn, unfortunately so misunderstand it they never recover. But this happens; for example, a few years ago I was at the US Army's West Point to see a football game with a friend who was then a professor at West Point, when he told me a very sad story. He had run into a freshman off campus. She had been dressed as a civilian. This is against the rules for a plebe. He saw her and she dashed away. He wasn't certain she was a freshman and didn't know her name, but he thought she was. That evening, she came to his home and asked him—he was a major in the Army at the time—not to report her. The cadet code is very simple. It goes: "A cadet will not lie, cheat, steal, or tolerate those who do." It was one thing to be caught breaking the rules. She would have been punished for that; perhaps she would have been sentenced to spending hours marching with a rifle around a flagpole. (As a cadet at Norwich University, I had to do that enough to put a dent in my right shoulder.) It was another thing to ask an officer to lie for her. He had no choice but to report her, and she was quickly expelled from the academy. Not tossing her out would have undermined the entire code everyone there lives by. She gave the Army no choice because she didn't understand the code—she thought she was still in high school.

It can be hard for someone entering a rite of passage from a morally relative society to understand how rigid a real code of honor can be. There is also no way to define philosophically every rule and how it applies to every situation in any code of honor. Philosophers have been trying to do that since Socrates and before. This is why West Point's simple code is brilliant for its brevity. It is easy to remember, and it rules out passive injustice by forcing anyone living under it not to "tolerate those" who lie, cheat, or steal. Imagine if lawyers and politicians weren't permitted to "tolerate those" who lie, cheat, or steal—what a world that would be.

Take this is a step further and think of a ballplayer who knows he was tagged out but play-acts to make a referee think he is safe anyway. Now, many fans want him to be safe either way and they won't ridicule him for trying to deceive, but just imagine if a baseball player said, "No, ump, he had me." Some fans would hiss and a baseball manager might lose his temper, but the act would resonate; it might even make the ballplayer famous; it might make their name synonymous with integrity. It would be that surprising and it would be honorable, something we all intuitively understand.

Perhaps that's too idealistic, but that's what codes of honor are.

Many codes are also very fundamental. The code between rock climbers, for example, is about life and death. Tying those knots properly and behaving in a responsible way can mean life or death to yourself and the rest of the people on the rope with you. In different ways, the same can be said about the codes firemen, police officers, doctors, and others follow. The rules are there for practical reasons, but when understood and followed they also lead to real honor, especially for those brave enough not to live one way on the job and another way when they're off.

What we can and must do is to read and ponder a code. (This is why I placed some profound ones as an appendix to this book.) As you look at the rules for the US Marine Corps, for cowboys, or even for the running of the bulls, you need to ask yourself why the rules were created. As you question them, you'll learn how to apply them and then how to live up to them—and if you want to live up to them, as not all codes are equal or even relevant to your life.

As you do, you'll find that without honor, all the good in any rite of passage falls away and all that's left is empty bravado.

STEP 6

The Reckoning

The feeling of commiseration is the beginning of humanity; the feeling of shame and dislike is the beginning of righteousness; the feeling of deference and compliance is the beginning of propriety; and the feeling of right and wrong is the beginning of wisdom. Men have these four beginnings just as they have their four limbs. Having these four beginnings, but saying that they cannot develop them is to destroy themselves.

—Mencius, China, third century B.C.

WITH A SPRINTER'S SURGE, I pushed though waves of tripping, panicked runners and ran for a hundred feet under the buildings towering five and six stories like walls with the bulls beside me on Estafeta and all the other runners pushing, shoving around me. I was in sync with the bulls' momentum, and all the other runners and the singing and shouting fell away into my pounding breath and beating heart. The moment slowed. I could feel the motion around me. I was with the bulls and their wild natures for two hundred feet—forever when you're in the street. The bulls had accepted all the people running with them, as they often do near the end of the course, and people were putting their hands softly on the bulls' black backs.

Getting to this place took stepping out of myself and letting an ideal take over. It took a suspension of the imagination to become that aesthetic bull runner in motion. It took not thinking too much as I found myself in the flow of the street and found a gap to get close to the bulls, and it took running for sheer joy.

Then I was jarred out of the moment by a runner stepping on my right heel and sending my sneaker flying off. I kept running with the bulls for another hundred feet but was out of step, distracted by my shoeless foot, and I no longer could see in my mind where all the bulls were. I pulled off past the turn onto Tramo de Telefonica that leads into the bullring and let the waves of runners pass me by, some bounced into me along the fence, as they pursued the bulls and then ran panicked again when the second set of steers came to sweep in any lone bull that might be left on the course.

When things go well, the euphoria lasts. I was still alive and unharmed and had run with wild bulls for a long stretch. I've had other moments of reckoning in the boxing ring and in nature with a fly rod or a bow in my hand, but it's the same harmony that comes from being in step with nature, with yourself, with life.

You're suddenly not in yourself but are everywhere in the moment. What has gotten you there is the driving simplicity of an icon, something that epitomizes a true role and you in step with that perfection. This is what the Japanese call Zen. In this case, I felt the part of the bull runner come into me and we ran together, but the moment was fleeting. This is the central reason I'm drawn back.

But that's only the nirvana of being in sync perfectly with the real action of a moment. The true reckoning is the realization. Few get close to articulating this. No one can completely for anyone but themselves, as these are personal experiences. For me, I was the bull and he was me. Living with that understanding—at least as much as that's possible—is what creates a truly great athlete or artist. It can make their triumphs shine for brief moments in a moving life. This is the power that can make someone come to life in a boardroom or on a basketball court. It is living the image personified. But the image isn't a facade. It's a pathway to the unexplainable, to the mystery of manly conduct that can only really be explained in the context of very specific happenings.

✳✳✳

After this splendid run, I decided I was ready to do the "suicide run" with Juan. In the suicide run, you start at the very beginning. Police block you from going farther than a green line painted on the street. Before the bulls come, the cops escape through a gap in a fence and you run at the bulls before dodging out of their way.

I was right in front, looking downhill about seventy-five yards to where the bulls would pound out of their pen on the right side of the narrow street. On my left was a retaining wall. On my right was a wooden fence. There are two sections of fence with about ten feet between them. In between the fences is where the police and medical workers stand. The police would arrest and fine us if we ran forward beyond a red line painted on the pavement. The medical workers were there to save our lives. People were sitting all along the outside fence and on top of the twenty-foot-high retaining wall. Runners were shoulder-to-shoulder with me and filling the street behind and uphill.

Just behind us, and up in a recess in the wall on Cuesta de Santo Domingo, a procession had placed a statue of San Fermín, as they do every morning just before the run, and had sung a song asking the saint to keep the runners safe and to help them be courageous under pressure.

When the police officers stepped out of the street, the one hundred runners at this very beginning of the course all turned away from where the bulls would soon come from and faced the small statue of San Fermín. I turned with them. With copies of newspapers rolled in our hands—it is popular to run with a copy of *Diario de Navarra* rolled in your hand, but any newspaper will do—we chanted: *"A San Fermín pedimos, por ser nuestro patron, nos guie en el encierro dandonos su bendicion."* (We ask San Fermín, being our patron saint, to guide us in the bull run and give us his blessing.) We chanted this three times as we shook our newspapers together at each syllable in the beat. When we finished we shouted "Viva San Fermín! Gora San Fermín!"

When we had done this, a newscaster with a position above shouted to ask if we would please do it again, as she hadn't gotten the chant on film. Everyone waiting for the bulls to come in seconds laughed and, perhaps because she was so attractive, did as she wished.

Then the rocket went up and we saw the gate to the pen bang open. The steers, white and brown, came out first. The bells on their necks were ringing. Two of the black bulls pushed past the steers, and they were all stampeding uphill for us. We had seconds. I ran forward, intensely watching the bulls. I had to decide whether to go right or left. Typically Juan goes right, as the fence at least offers an escape. But where you go depends on where the bulls are. In this place there can be no hesitation. Hesitating will get you run over, maybe gored.

The bulls were spread out across the street. Neither side seemed better than the other. I went right.

A bull broke to take the far right side. He was turning his head to hook us with his sharp, forward-facing horns. His horns were black with ivory-collared tips. They seemed to float along like spears in slow motion.

At this first section on the course, the bulls are not yet used to people being in the street with them. Here they can be very aggressive. Though they are typically just being defensive.

What often saves people on Santo Domingo is that the bulls are going very fast on this first uphill section of street. The bulls rarely stop here. If they get someone, they get them while running almost full out.

I went flat against the fence. In the fragments of that speedy moment, I remember seeing this stomach protecting me.

A man on my right as I stood with my back against the fence and closer to the hooking bull had a gut that stuck out well past mine. He had a great watermelon of a stomach. The bull swung at him and the fat man all but fell over on me and somehow the bull missed and pounded past. The man with the stomach went down on one knee as he took a great breath and looked at the pavement. He'd come within a few inches of being gutted. I'd only come within inches of having that man's guts on me.

It was good I'd run many times, and had some fine runs, before the suicide run with Juan. I'd learned poise with the bulls, even to suspend my imagination. I'd learned to let the iconic bull runner invade me and sweep me into safety.

We walked back up the street. Somewhere on toward the arena the bulls were still running. The bulls would put eight people in the hospital that day, but none would be hurt very seriously.

Pamplona's San Fermín festival has a way of mixing in a little absurdity, as if just to add flavor to the brew, so we were hardly surprised to see a little drama of a different kind taking place on Santo Domingo. Two men were trying to help a woman. She was a large woman who had somehow crawled over a metal rail to sit on the top of a fifteen-foot-high retaining wall overlooking the bull run. She had sat there so long—getting a spot to watch the run is always competitive—that she had lost feeling in her dangling legs and needed to be lifted up and back over the rail. The two men needed the help of a third, and pretty soon there was a crowd pulling her back up and over. They almost lost her and those below dodged away, none wanting to sacrifice themselves for her. On the third heave they hoisted her over and she fell on them and everyone was laughing.

Having a close call with a bull heightens everything.

What's more difficult is retaining this connection. Not that such an ideal should completely define someone, as that is too simplistic a way to be, but when you understand there is an ideal you can be, can even rely upon at the hardest times, then things get clearer, simpler, as you know how to become more than yourself. You know that anyone who can do such things can keep their head in a crisis.

This is, of course, the pursuit of an ideal. And at this point you find that ultimately a guide to boot camp isn't a drill instructor, a guide to a football game isn't a coach, and my guide to running with the bulls wasn't Juan Macho. The real guide is the ideal these people represent and, as much as they can, live up to. The ideal isn't real. It is something apart from us that can help us. Realizing this idealized role is not you, but is there to help you, is essential. It is also a fading conception.

The author Elizabeth Gilbert pointed out in a TED Talk that the Ancient Greeks thought that genius comes to us as a muse; they thought that divine things influence our greatest minds. The Ancient Greeks thought some people could hear their muses clearer than others or that some people just had better muses. The Ancient Romans called these influential muses *"genius,"* but not in the modern sense. In ancient Rome, a *genius* was a guiding spirit. Some talented people were thought to have particularly powerful *geniuses* whispering deep thoughts in their ears. Later, during the Enlightenment, came rational humanism, which dispelled this notion of muses and said it was really the person, and not some fairy with pixie dust or something, that was the genius. And so we lost a useful metaphor and became burdened with the idea we can be fools or geniuses. That's a lot of weight to put on any person. Gilbert pointed out that the old way, though a fanciful way of looking at where inspiration and new ideas come from, had its advantages, as a person wouldn't constantly have to live up to an unrealistic label.

A similar thing has happened to our view of ideal figures. Today we more often view them as too simplistic. While it's true that such archetypes are simplistic and that no one could really be as perfect as the mythologized Roland or the Christopher Reeve version of Superman in all the scenes of their lives, isn't it useful to have an ideal to measure ourselves against? If instead of only thinking self-centrically, even egotistically, about the good and bad parts of our natures, habits, and biases as we try to improve ourselves, if we instead entertain the idea we're chasing archetypes—not real, but still guiding lights of perfection—into our pursuits to become whatever we're drawn to be, wouldn't we have a better chance of getting closer to the ideal?

For Hemingway, beyond the Christian ideals in the background, the iconic figure in *The Sun Also Rises* is the bullfighter, not the bull runner. In the novel his name is Pedro Romero. In his earliest draft of the novel, Hemingway named this character Cayetano Ordóñez, the real name of a young bullfighter Hemingway saw in 1925.[1] Hemingway

---

[1] H. R. Stoneback, *Reading Hemingway's The Sun Also Rises*, The Kent State University Press, Kent, Ohio, 2007.

then changed the name to Antonio Guerra, which is close to the name of a famed nineteenth-century matador. But then he settled on Pedro Romero. This is thought to be because Hemingway was naming him after Pedro Romero Martínez (1754–1839). Pedro Romero Martínez was a legendary bullfighter from the Romero family in Ronda, Spain. His grandfather, Francisco, is credited with advancing the art of using the muleta; his father and two of his brothers were also toreros. As a youth, Pedro Romero Martínez participated in bullfights in Algeciras and in Seville in 1772 and in Madrid in 1775. In the following year, he killed 285 bulls, establishing his reputation. He allegedly fought 5,558 bulls without incurring serious injury before retiring in 1799. He was known as the first matador to present the bullfight as an art form as well as a display of courage.

✳✳✳

Stoneback notes that Pedro Romero is actually the "core image" of the novel.[2] Romero is first introduced in a mostly dark room with a "little light" coming in where the young bullfighter sits in his white linen and seems "very far away and dignified" and "straight and handsome and altogether by himself." Stoneback compares this image to one of "a little girl with muddy drawers up in a tree" William Faulkner used as the cornerstone for his novel *The Sound and the Fury*. Stoneback says that the "first sentence of Hemingway's first draft was about Romero: 'I saw him for the first time in his room

---

[2]Ibid.

at the Hotel Quintana in Pamplona.'" Stoneback argues that Hemingway actually built the entire novel, the whole pilgrimage with Jake and the others from the Lost Generation, around the core image of this young, idealized bullfighter.

By doing so, Hemingway wanted to show a better way. Stoneback told me, "Hemingway stresses Romero's sense of his craft, his art, its separateness from personality. Like a true artist, Romero's art has nothing to do with the merely personal; it exists in the dimension of technique, tradition, and passion—not ego."

This is likely why Romero isn't a complete character in the novel. He is a young, simple painting of an idealized character. He is all that a bullfighter should be and nothing he shouldn't be. He almost isn't human. He represents the paradigm bullfighters try to attain in the arena.

When Romero fights a bull in the novel, Hemingway describes him as acting "smoothly, calmly, and beautifully." He says that all of Romero's passes with the cape and the charging bull are "linked up, all completed, all slow, tempered and smooth."

A more complete explanation of how Hemingway sees the ideal bullfighter can be found in his book *Death in the Afternoon*. Hemingway says that in those great moments, a bullfighter has "valor, art, understanding and, above all, beauty and great emotion." To describe this idealized matador, Hemingway uses the Spanish word *pundonor*, which he defines as "honor, probity, courage, self-respect, and pride."

Hemingway, in *Death in the Afternoon*, addresses the doubt likely held by an American audience to this description by saying, "It is impossible to believe the emotional and spiritual intensity and pure, classic beauty that can be produced by a man, an animal, and a piece of scarlet serge draped over a stick. If you do not choose to believe it possible and want to regard it all as nonsense you may be able to prove you are right by going to a bullfight in which nothing magical occurs; and there are many of them. . . . But if you should ever see the real thing you would know it."

Each afternoon, after running with the bulls, we'd go to see the bulls we ran with die at the hands of a matador trying to be this masculine ideal—and often failing.

Now, before getting into that, I should say that a bullfight can be a difficult thing to watch. I think they should be a difficult thing to watch. Still, without the bullfights, the run with the bulls would lose its significance; it would cease to exist. The San Fermín festival would wither and die without the reality of real bulls and death within it. Some would like this to happen. I can sympathize, even at times side, with that viewpoint when it's held by an educated person, by someone who has really tried to understand the bullfight.

When Professor Allen Josephs, who teaches literature at the University of West Florida in Pensacola and is the author of *On Hemingway and Spain*, was asked if "ultimately bullfighting symbolizes whatever needs to be symbolized" for the person watching the tragedy, Josephs said, "No. I find that sort of relativism avoids the real issue, which is the deep meaning of *toreo*, a ritual sacrifice that recapitulates the oldest myths and rituals we have. Much as in the Mass. You can say that the wafer and the wine symbolize whatever we need for it to symbolize, but in fact it doesn't symbolize anything. It is. Nor does the *corrida* symbolize anything. It is. In fact, and I do mean fact, it is the non-symbolic nature of the *corrida* that is important. The bulls are very real—real fear, real danger, real force, real pain, real blood, real death. The realest thing in the world. And the less we live in reality (instead of virtual reality) the more vital the reality of the ring becomes. There is no otherness quite like the bull. Ortega y Gasset tells the story of the matador who was being heckled by a famous actor, safe in his seat. Finally the matador, *Cúchares*, said to the actor with his finest Andalusian scorn: 'Down here you don't just die a make-believe death like you do in the theater!'"

To add basis to this point, Josephs said, "[W]hat I am about to say will perplex some—and that is that to be a real [bullfight] aficionado, you must love animals, and especially the bull. Killing what we love, eating what we love, making rituals and religions to atone for that paradox seem to be a permanent fixture as far back as we can trace human behavior. The real aficionado is in search of one of mankind's oldest and deepest mysteries. Some people get it and some don't. Those that don't, however, have no right to suppose that they are on the moral high ground and even less to try to impose their criteria on others. That's cultural fascism, no matter how well intended or high minded."

This is why Josephs thinks the bullfight will soon be done away with. He said, "The politically correct fascists will not let it live. The modern world is so full of fear and hatred and control that it cannot let something which it cannot comprehend exist. It's all about non-loving, non-spiritual control and power. But that attitude is also killing education, religion and a host of other things. Hemingway knew it, Faulkner did, [Cormac] McCarthy does."[3]

The bullfight's reverie is certainly just as hard to understand as the hero shot of a hunter is for someone who doesn't hunt. There is this hunter smiling with this just-killed and once-beautiful animal. How is someone who has never hunted supposed to understand the hunter's joy? A person who doesn't hunt can be understandably appalled by the elation on the face of a hunter who has just killed. Many feel the same way about the bullfighters strutting like peacocks after they go over the horns to thrust swords into bulls. Revulsion to these images and acts is why a number of animal-rights groups, such as Antitauromaquia and StopOurShame, protest the bullfights in Spain, southern France, and in other countries.

At my first bullfight, I was in tears watching a bull bleed and be killed and was saying as much to a friend. An elderly Spanish woman who'd been sharing her wine and pastries with us before the bullfight overheard me and saw my eyes and said with disgust, "You Americans are so soft. You're supposed to be hunters and cold *capitalistas*, yet you can't stand to see a matador and a bull face their lives together in celebration of life."

She misjudged me. I am a hunter and I eat what I kill. I understand that anyone who eats is a part of this process. I know that even a vegetarian can't opt out, as the farmers who raise the vegetables they eat still have to control, often with

---

[3]www.thehemingwayproject.com/category/allen-josephs/.

lethal means, the insects, birds, deer, geese, mice, or whatever might feed on their crops. If a farmer doesn't protect his crops, in the end, all he or she will be doing is raising crops for wildlife.

The bulls killed in the arena are all also eaten. I've witnessed them being butchered in a cement room in the Plaza de Toros in Pamplona, and I've eaten meat from the bulls served at local restaurants that I've run with and have seen die in the arena.

Also, the Spanish will tell you that a bull has a chance to be pardoned. They call this *indulto*. If a bull is especially brave, nearly fearless, and runs true. The audience may begin to chant *indulto* and the judges for the fight might spare the bull. This is seen as a great honor for the bull's breeder. A bull that is pardoned will go back to the ranch and will spend its years siring cows. But an *indulto* is very rare—too rare to justify anything that happens in the arena.

Others, such as the author Alexander Fiske-Harrison, a man who trained as a bullfighter to research a book, argued: "In terms of animal welfare, the fighting bull lives four to six years whereas the meat cow lives one to two. What is more, it doesn't just live in the sense of existing, it lives a full and natural life. Those years are spent free, roaming in the *dehesa*, the lightly wooded natural pastureland which is the residue of the ancient forests of Spain. It is a rural idyll, although with the modern additions of full veterinary care and an absence of predators big enough to threaten evolution's answer to a main battle tank."[4]

---

[4]Alexander Fiske-Harrison, *Into the Arena: The World of the Spanish Bullfight*, Profile Books, London, 2011.

Still others defend the death of the bull by pointing out that the death of animals in slaughterhouses is often much worse than the death in the ring, and that at least a bull has a chance to kill the matador. Still, selling tickets to the slaying of an animal is hard to defend. Even Hemingway said he wouldn't defend it. Hemingway wrote, "I won't defend the bullfight. It isn't a sport. It's a tragedy in three acts."[5]

I accept the bullfight because I've found that this choreographed tragedy is symbolic of the hunt, of facing our mortality and coming to terms with our nourishment. At its essence it is actually a very honest thing. I asked Juan about this and he said, "Yes, it is so. We need to understand our connection to the natural world. It's not just out there, but also in our flesh. People today have often lost touch with this connection to where their sustenance comes from. The bullfighters, however, know this well. They live on the razor's edge of this truth. They stand toe-to-hoof with this reality as men once did to secure meat."

The central problem most people have with the bullfight is that it puts this connection to our sustenance on display. As it does so, it glorifies this connection and idealizes the men who kill well and beautifully. Those who see this as an honorable death for the bull, and possibly for the matador, don't have a problem with bullfighting. Those who see this public death of the bull, and possible goring or death of the bullfighter, as appalling have a genuine reason for opposing bullfighting.

After a personal struggle with bullfighting—long after I struggled with whether hunting is right in today's world—I

---

[5]Ernest Hemingway, *Death in the Afternoon*, Scribner's, New York, 1932.

came to the conclusion that reality shouldn't be completely hidden from us. We need reality as our basis in order to grow into honest and mature people. To be all we can be, we need to understand and respect where our food comes from. We need to understand that we are part of the natural system, not apart from it. Glorifying this connection with a bear rug on the floor or with a bullfight are complex things but not wrong, in my judgment, as long as the hunter or matador shows respect for the animals they kill.

When bullfighting is a part of someone's culture—as it had been for that elderly Spanish lady at the Plaza de Toros in Pamplona—it is easier to accept. For me, it is always emotional. It is especially hard to watch when the matador fails to kill cleanly. The audience doesn't like this, either. They begin to hiss. If the matador fails to kill the bull with the sword on several attempts, the bullfight fans will start to throw their seat cushions. If it drags on too long, the officials will embarrass the matador by ending the fight.

I find it good that bullfight fans cheer when a matador kills a bull quickly and cleanly, and that they get angry when he doesn't. They want a clean kill, and that's a respectful way to be.

I've seen this in hunting camps. If someone comes back to camp after wounding an animal, the other hunters are different around him. They treat him like he is a contagious person, like a leper. I've seen men opt not to sit with such a person at dinner. This isn't taught and is rarely talked about among men. It has always seemed to me to be a very natural reaction.

In 2015 in Pamplona's Plaza de Toros, I saw two bullfights, back-to-back, that showcased this. Juan José Padilla, the Cyclone of Jerez, thirty-eight years old, father of two, and a crowd favorite who had come out of retirement, couldn't kill his bull. He went in with the sword over the horns but stuck the sword in too high. He didn't get the bull's heart or even its lungs. The audience grew quiet. Even the peña's marching bands, who are always loud from the sunny side of Pamplona's bullring, went silent. They wanted this matador with the weathered face, with the eye lost to a bull at Zaragoza, who had represented the ideal so many times in the arena, to kill well. He didn't, and the eyes all around me were moist and heads drooped. Padilla looked deeply embarrassed.

This changed when one of the other matadors, Alberto Lopez Simon, fought his bulls. The young bullfighter might have been Pedro Romero that day. His passes were close and his movement little. He strutted yet tenderly placed his hand on the bull as it gasped its last breaths. He had *pundonor*. The judges gave him two ears. A teenage girl sitting with her father and mother in front of me was swooning for him. Simon bowed to the audience in his "suit of lights" (*traje de luces*), a custom-made and tight suit that's embroidered with silver or golden thread. He was the ideal image personified. Only a matador who won at least two ears is given permission to be carried on the shoulders of the admirers (*salida en hombros*), and this young bullfighter received that honor to a long standing ovation.

The bullfighter and the audience understood the ideal Hemingway was using as his ideal man in *The Sun Also Rises*. Whatever anyone thinks of bullfighting, the bullfighter lives boldly in the ring. What he does in the arena is, at its most extreme, what men once had to do to kill game to feed their brethren. They had to kill or die.

But this is only one ideal from a particular culture. At the basis of others societies, cultures, and subcultures are priests, soldiers, sports stars, firefighters, and so many more. Any real rite of passage, whether it be rock climbing or seminary school, has an archetype as its guiding light. As Floyd Patterson once told me, understanding this helps us achieve the ideal.

So can you handle being possessed? Can you play this part all the way? There is a danger here, too. There is a smugness, too much pride. This is never a simple thing. You have to continue to try to understand and to be humble within the bounds of the ideal.

STEP 7

THE WAY

To practice Zen or the Martial Arts, you must live intensely, whole-heartedly, without reserve, as if you might die in the next instant.

—Taisen Deshimaru

AFTER MIDNIGHT ON JULY 14, a dozen men and women were kneeling along a wall with lighted white candles clenched in their hands. They were on a side street, just off Santa Domingo on the beginning of the bull run. An American woman was on her knees sobbing as her gray hair stuck to her face. Her adult daughter was kneeling beside her with her arm around her mother's convulsing shoulders. A man from Detroit I'd seen loud and drunk day and night was leaning his forehead into the wall and crying as wax from his candle dripped down the wall and mingled with the wax from other candles. A French photographer was taking photos with his lens too close to the dozen people crying along the wall. No one acknowledged he was there with his flash strumming.

Within arm's reach of these mourning people were dozens of others laughing, telling stories with bottles of half-drunk wine in their hands in this half-lighted alley.

"Remember how he came up this street right on the horns—"

"And then he fell."

"Yeah, but he didn't just fall. He dove and slid on his face and the bull just glanced at him."

"I've seen the video so many times. The bull actually looked sorry for him."

The woman who'd been sobbing uncontrollably stood and said, "He could be such a clown, but he was my clown."

One of the men laughing with a bottle of wine in his hand gave the red wine to the woman who'd lost her husband. She took a long swig with the bottle tipped all the way up. Before she was done, the man who'd given her the bottle was kneeling in front of the wall like a Catholic and crying as he prayed.

This is the "wailing wall." The place runners come to mourn those they've lost, not just in the street, but in life. This wall isn't just for the few killed or wounded on the streets with the bulls. This is for the people who came and ran and entered this group of people who are drawn to this place and to this primal celebration of life amidst death. The mourners kept talking about friends lost; people they connected with in Pamplona. This place was a closer connection to these lost souls than any gravestone or hometown. It is where they came together in the depths of something profound. It is where they were honest and full of joy.

We'd come down to this wall after midnight and after the festival's closing ceremony. We'd come from the square in front of the ornate town hall where this festival begins and ends. The square had been full. After nine days of partying, many meet in the City Hall Plaza at midnight on July 14. The square fills but is not so full as for the opening celebration at noon on July 6.

At midnight everyone sings the traditional mournful notes of *"Pobre de Mí"* (Poor Me) in a candlelit ending. Pamplona's mayor closes the festival and everyone lights a candle and removes their red handkerchiefs as the song is played by a local band and everyone sings again and again in mournful notes: *"Pobre de Mí, Pobre de Mí, que se han acabado las fiestas, de San Fermín."* (Poor me, poor me, for the fiesta of San Fermín has come to a close.) The tune is as cheery and blue as a New Orleans funeral procession.

Singing this song with thousands after so many days spent with bulls and in the fiesta's celebration carried people into a religious ecstasy, as we held candles and our red bandannas up and lamented the passing of another San Fermín festival and looked forward to the next. There are other events taking place in the city, such as the peñas gathering in the main square, the Plaza del Castillo, for their own celebration. This is a sad occasion, as it is the end of the fiesta. Still, many also sing *"Ya falta menos"* (There is not long to go) until the next fiesta.

Some stubbornly continue partying through the night despite the fact that the city is succumbing to its normal rhythm. Bar after bar pulls down its shutters. In the early morning light these last lonely revelers seem out of place on the quiet streets. A few will move on and run in the *encierro de la villavesa* or another Spanish festival where the bulls run down streets to an arena.

We pulled away from the wall as others arrived, and we walked downhill on Santa Domingo in the darkness cut only by a few yellow streetlights.

We stopped under the retaining wall where the tiny statue of San Fermín sits fifteen feet up. There were photos taken, and then this twenty-four-year-old English girl, a daughter of one of the longtime runners, apologized for having Pamplona throat before she sang Sting's "Fields of Gold." She paused once as a group of tall and lean Spanish police officers passed between us on the narrow street and someone shouted in English "thank you, *gracias, gracias.* . . ." The officers were amused and embarrassed.

We had our arms on one another's shoulders then, and most of us were lightly drunk from wine and very drunk with emotion.

Like any rite of passage, this one ends when you are ceremonially accepted among men of honor in a unit, team, company, firehouse, or dojo. You enter a guarded society, a fraternity of men. As you do, you also know that at any time the archetype you are trying to live up to will abandon you if you break the code, that to be all you can be, you must live up to something other than yourself.

J. J., a heart surgeon who has become the charismatic leader of Juan's peña, led us down the street to the pen where the bulls are held for the night before they run the course to the arena. The pen isn't much bigger than the average American's living room. In the dark, it felt ominous and smelled like a dairy barn. We lined up along the walls and peed in the pen. As we did, the doctor said, "Bulls, we survived you another year. Thank you for sharing your lives, your power, with us. By pissing where you did we let you know we survived and will be back again to celebrate life with you."

As a dozen of us walked back up the dark street, the doctor said, "Juan created that little ritual out of respect. We're men together now in something bigger than ourselves."

The way in *The Sun Also Rises* is the end. Jake's baptism from the novel's debauchery comes when he swims by himself in the Bay of Biscay. This prepares him for the last scene, when Lady Brett summons him to Madrid. He takes a ride in a taxi with her, and Lady Brett says, "Oh, Jake, we could have had such a damned good time together." Jakes replies, "Yes, isn't it pretty to think so." He is at peace with his situation. It's hard to believe he could have gotten to that place without the pilgrimage from Paris to Pamplona.

So I found along the way that my question about what makes men is actually something many ancient cultures answered in the same way. The Aztecs, Cherokee, Spartans, Romans, Jews, Maasai . . . all created ritualized rites of passage to make sure their youth grew into men who benefit the tribe, clan, or city. Some mutilated their own bodies. Some fasted and prayed by themselves in the wilderness. One tribe in the South Pacific still jumps from towers with vines attached to their feet. The Amazon's Satere Mawé tribe still requires boys as young as twelve years old to repeatedly wear ceremonial gloves filled with venomous bullet ants. More modern rites of passage psychologically tear down recruits before building them into soldiers, firemen, and police officers. Another sends people running before the horns of bulls, while another places people on the backs of bulls. All of these rites of passage have wildly different rituals, but they all also follow the same general rules, the same guidelines for creating mature people that gave this book its structure.

Incredibly, ancient cultures all over the world independently came to the conclusion that maturity can't be left to chance. They found that growing older doesn't by itself make people into valuable members of a society. They learned that repelling invaders, being successful in the hunt, having honorable citizens, and more require generations of mature members who can be counted on to be honorable and courageous citizens. So they created rites of passage, ritualized adventures filled with physical and psychological obstacles, to evolve boys into mature adults—that is, if they passed, which has never been a sure thing with any real rite of passage.

As Floyd Patterson showed, the rites of passage we chose are not about our gender, color, looks, or nationality. No, each depends on us. Real rites of passage are always there ready to redeem us and carry us forward. They make us better, which is why cultures often presented a series of trials to members as they grew older.

What makes men, as it turns out, is a selfless connection to a real code of honor. How can any of us do such a thing? We must understand and follow a real rite of passage, and not just one, but new ones in each chapter of our lives. That's the key.

That's what has always shaped men into men. That is why a wise man learns the world isn't all about him, that there is something greater than himself. Understanding that there is something greater than the self doesn't diminish the self. When properly in step, it makes a man as large as the solar system.

APPENDIX

Codes of Honor

To LIVE WITH HONOR, WE need a code, basic guidelines to keep us on the right course in the gray areas of life. The best way to do this is to read codes of honor from both ancient cultures and modern institutions while asking ourselves what rules we should live by. From that inquest will come revelations and answers. Here are some good codes of honor to begin with.

The Golden Rule

The Bible defines the "golden rule" as "Do unto others as you would have them do unto you."[1] In the first century BC, around the same time Cicero was writing *De Officiis,* a book written to teach his son to be a man by following a code, Rabbi Hillel, a renowned Jewish religious leader, said, "That which is hateful to you, do not do to your fellow; that is the

---

[1] New Testament, Matthew 7:12.

whole Torah; the rest is the explanation; go and learn."[2] The Golden Rule is the foundation of any real code of honor. Fake codes, such as those maintained by some gangs, set themselves apart from the Golden Rule by deciding they only have to honor those in their gang, group, or religion. Real codes of honor treat every person—whatever their creed, color, race, or background—according to the same values we live by.

Scout Oath (or Promise) of the Boy Scouts of America

"On my honor, I will do my best to do my duty to God and my country and to obey the Scout Law; to help other people at all times; to keep myself physically strong, mentally awake, and morally straight."

The Ten Commandments

The Bible's Old Testament tells us Moses brought these ten rules down from Mount Sinai, directly from God. They are still the Western foundation of morality.

1. I am the LORD your God who brought you out of the land of Egypt, from the house of slavery. You shall have no other gods before Me.
2. Do not make an image or any likeness of what is in the heavens above.

---

[2] *Babylonian Talmud*, tractate Shabbat 31a.

3. Do not swear falsely by the name of the LORD.
4. Remember the Sabbath day and keep it holy.
5. Honor your father and your mother.
6. Do not murder.
7. Do not commit adultery.
8. Do not steal.
9. Do not bear false witness against your neighbor.
10. Do not covet your neighbor's wife.

The US Military Academy's Creed

A Cadet will not lie, cheat, or steal, nor tolerate those who do.

Hinduism's Basic Codes

The Ten Yamas (Restraints)

Yama 1: Ahimsa (Non-injury): Practice non-injury, not harming others by thought, word or deed, even in your dreams. Live a kindly life, revering all beings as expressions of the One Divine energy. Let go of fear and insecurity, the sources of abuse. Knowing that harm caused to others unfailingly returns to oneself, live peacefully with God's creation. Never be a source of dread, pain, or injury. Follow a vegetarian diet.

Yama 2: Satya (Truthfulness): Adhere to truthfulness, refraining from lying and betraying promises. Speak only that which is true, kind, helpful, and necessary. Knowing that deception creates distance, don't keep secrets from family or loved ones. Be fair, accurate, and frank in discussions, a stranger to deceit.

Admit your failings. Do not engage in slander, gossip, or back-biting. Do not bear false witness against another.

Yama 3: Asteya (Nonstealing): Uphold the virtue of non-stealing, neither thieving, coveting, nor failing to repay debt. Control your desires and live within your means. Do not use borrowed resources for unintended purposes or keep them past due. Do not gamble or defraud others. Do not renege on promises. Do not use others' name, words, resources, or rights without permission and acknowledgement.

Yama 4: Brahmacharya (Divine Conduct): Practice divine conduct, controlling lust by remaining celibate when single and faithful in marriage. Before marriage, use vital energies in study, and after marriage in creating family success. Don't waste the sacred force by promiscuity in thought, word, or deed. Be restrained with the opposite sex. Seek holy company. Dress and speak modestly. Shun pornography, sexual humor, and violence.

Yama 5: Kshama (Patience): Exercise patience, restraining from intolerance with people and impatience with circum-stances. Be agreeable. Let others behave according to their nature, without adjusting to you. Don't argue, dominate con-versations, or interrupt others. Don't be in a hurry. Be patient with children and the elderly. Minimize stress by keeping worries at bay. Remain poised in good times and bad.

Yama 6: Dhriti (Steadfastness): Foster steadfastness, over-coming non perseverance, fear, indecision, and change-ableness. Achieve your goals with a prayer, purpose, plan, persistence, and push. Be firm in your decisions. Avoid sloth and procrastination. Develop willpower, courage, and industriousness. Overcome obstacles. Never carp or complain. Do not let opposition or fear of failure result in changing strategies.

Yama 7: Daya (Compassion): Practice compassion, conquering callous, cruel, and insensitive feelings toward all beings. See God everywhere. Be kind to people, animals, plants, and the Earth itself. Forgive those who apologize and show true remorse. Foster sympathy for others' needs and suffering. Honor and assist those who are weak, impoverished, aged, or in pain. Oppose family abuse and other cruelties.

Yama 8: Arjava (Honesty): Maintain honesty, renouncing deception and wrongdoing. Act honorably even in hard times. Obey the laws of your nation and locale. Pay your taxes. Be straightforward in business. Do an honest day's work. Do not bribe or accept bribes. Do not cheat, deceive, or circumvent to achieve an end. Be frank with yourself. Face and accept your faults without blaming them on others.

Yama 9: Mitahara (Moderate Appetite): Be moderate in appetite, neither eating too much nor consuming meat, fish, shellfish, fowl, or eggs. Enjoy fresh, wholesome vegetarian foods that vitalize the body. Avoid junk food. Drink in moderation. Eat at regular times, only when hungry, at a moderate pace, never between meals, in a disturbed atmosphere, or when upset. Follow a simple diet, avoiding rich or fancy fare.

Yama 10: Saucha (Purity): Uphold the ethic of purity, avoiding impurity in mind, body, and speech. Maintain a clean, healthy body. Keep a pure, uncluttered home and workplace.

Act virtuously. Keep good company, never mixing with adulterers, thieves, or other impure people. Keep away from pornography and violence. Never use harsh, angered, or indecent language. Worship devoutly. Meditate daily.

The 10 NiYama (Observances)

NiYama 1: Hri (Remorse): Allow yourself the expression of remorse, being modest, and showing shame for misdeeds. Recognize your errors, confess, and make amends. Sincerely apologize to those hurt by your words or deeds. Resolve all contention before sleep. Seek out and correct your faults and bad habits. Welcome correction as a means to bettering yourself. Do not boast. Shun pride and pretension.

NiYama 2: Santosha (Contentment): Nurture contentment, seeking joy, and serenity in life. Be happy, smile, and uplift others. Live in constant gratitude for your health, your friends, and your belongings. Don't complain about what you don't possess. Identify with the eternal You, rather than mind, body, or emotions. Keep the mountaintop view that life is an opportunity for spiritual progress. Live in the eternal now.

NiYama 3: Dana (Giving): Be generous to a fault, giving liberally without thought of reward. Tithe, offering one-tenth of your gross income (*dashamamsha*), as God's money, to temples, ashrams, and spiritual organizations. Approach the temple with offerings. Visit *guru* with gifts in hand.

Donate religious literature. Feed and give to those in need. Bestow your time and talents without seeking praise. Treat guests as God.

NiYama 4: Astikya (Faith): Cultivate an unshakable faith. Believe firmly in God, Gods, *guru*, and your path to enlightenment. Trust in the words of the masters, the scriptures, and traditions. Practice devotion and *sadhana* to inspire experiences that build advanced faith. Be loyal to your lineage, one with your *satguru*. Shun those who try to break your faith by argument and accusation. Avoid doubt and despair.

NiYama 5: Ishvarapujana (Worship): Cultivate devotion through daily worship and meditation. Set aside one room of your home as God's shrine. Offer fruit, flowers, or food daily. Learn a simple puja and the chants. Meditate after each puja. Visit your shrine before and after leaving the house. Worship in heartfelt devotion, clearing the inner channels to God, gods, and *guru* so their grace flows toward you and loved ones.

NiYama 6: Siddhanta Shravana (Scriptural Listening): Eagerly hear the scriptures, study the teachings and listen to the wise of your lineage. Choose a guru, follow his path, and don't waste time exploring other ways. Read, study and, above all, listen to readings and dissertations by which wisdom flows from knower to seeker. Avoid secondary texts that preach violence. Revere and study the revealed scriptures, the *Vedas* and *Agamas*.

NiYama7: Mati (Cognition): Develop a spiritual will and intellect with your *satguru's* guidance. Strive for knowledge of God, to awaken the light within. Discover the hidden lesson in each experience to develop a profound understanding of life and yourself. Through meditation, cultivate intuition by listening to the still, small voice within, by understanding the subtle sciences, inner worlds, and mystical texts.

NiYama 8: Vrata (Sacred Vows): Embrace religious vows, rules, and observances, and never waver in fulfilling them. Honor vows as spiritual contracts with your soul, your community, with God, gods, and *guru*. Take vows to harness the instinctive nature. Fast periodically. Pilgrimage yearly. Uphold your vows strictly, be they marriage, monasticism, non addiction, tithing, loyalty to a lineage, vegetarianism, or nonsmoking.

NiYama 9: Japa (Recitation): Chant your holy *mantra* daily, reciting the sacred sound, word, or phrase given by your guru. Bathe first, quiet the mind, and concentrate fully to let japa harmonize, purify and uplift you. Heed your instructions and chant the prescribed repetitions without fail. Live free of anger so that *japa* strengthens your higher nature. Let *japa* quell emotions and quiet the rivers of thought.

NiYama 10: Tapas (Austerity): Practice austerity, serious disciplines, penance, and sacrifice. Be ardent in worship, meditation, and pilgrimage. Atone for misdeeds through penance (*prayashchitta*), such as 108 prostrations or fasting. Perform self-denial, giving up cherished possessions, money, or time. Fulfill severe austerities at special times, under a *satguru's* guidance, to ignite the inner fires of self-transformation.

Buddhism's Eight Precepts[3]

Buddha taught the precepts to help men live free from guilt from wrongdoing, so that people can progress more easily on their path to enlightenment.

1. I undertake the training rule to abstain from taking life.
2. I undertake the training rule to abstain from taking what is not given.
3. I undertake the training rule to abstain from sexual misconduct.
4. I undertake the training rule to abstain from false speech.
5. I undertake the training rule to abstain from malicious speech.
6. I undertake the training rule to abstain from harsh speech.
7. I undertake the training rule to abstain from useless speech.
8. I undertake the training rule to abstain from drinks and drugs that cause heedlessness.

The Ten Precepts of Taoism[4]

The Ten Precepts are the classical rules of Chinese Taoism, a man's guide to justice and morality.

1. Do not kill but always be mindful of the host of living beings.
2. Do not be lascivious or think depraved thoughts.

---

[3]Bhante Gunaratana, "Taking the Eight Lifetime Precepts," Bhavana Society (www.bhavanasociety.org/resource/taking_the_eight_lifetme_precepts/).
[4]Livia Kohn, *Cosmos & Community: The Ethical Dimension of Daoism,* Three Pines Press, St. Petersburg, Florida, 2004.

3. Do not steal or receive unrighteous wealth.
4. Do not cheat or misrepresent good and evil.
5. Do not get intoxicated but always think of pure conduct.
6. I will maintain harmony with my ancestors and family and never disregard my kin.
7. When I see someone do a good deed, I will support him with joy and delight.
8. When I see someone unfortunate, I will support him with dignity to recover good fortune.
9. When someone comes to do me harm, I will not harbor thoughts of revenge.
10. As long as all beings have not attained the Tao, I will not expect to do so myself.

Benjamin Franklin's 13 Rules of Improvement

Franklin sought to cultivate his character and become a wise and just man by adhering to what he ascertained to be the fundamental 13 virtues. He first developed these when he was twenty years old (in 1726). He recorded them in his autobiography:

1. TEMPERANCE: Eat not to dullness; drink not to elevation.
2. SILENCE: Speak not but what may benefit others or yourself; avoid trifling conversation.
3. ORDER: Let all your things have their places; let each part of your business have its time.
4. RESOLUTION: Resolve to perform what you ought; perform without fail what you resolve.
5. FRUGALITY: Make no expense but to do good to others or yourself; i.e., waste nothing.

6. INDUSTRY: Lose no time; be always employed in something useful; cut off all unnecessary actions.
7. SINCERITY: Use no hurtful deceit; think innocently and justly, and, if you speak, speak accordingly.
8. JUSTICE: Wrong none by doing injuries, or omitting the benefits that are your duty.
9. MODERATION: Avoid extremes; forbear resenting injuries so much as you think they deserve.
10. CLEANLINESS: Tolerate no uncleanliness in body, clothes, or habitation.
11. TRANQUILITY: Be not disturbed at trifles, or at accidents common or unavoidable.
12. CHASTITY: Rarely use venery but for health or offspring, never to dullness, weakness, or the injury of your own or another's peace or reputation.
13. HUMILITY: Imitate Jesus and Socrates.

Tecumseh's Rules for Living

We remember Geronimo and Sitting Bull because they fought valiantly and lost in an age when the Native American had already become a romantically tragic figure. But we've forgotten Tecumseh, a Shawnee who almost halted what was later termed as "Manifest Destiny." He was a charismatic leader who united tribes in defense of an ancient way of life in the late eighteenth and early nineteenth centuries. Before he became the ninth president of the United States, William Henry Harrison wrote that Tecumseh is "one of those uncommon geniuses which spring up occasionally to produce revolutions and overturn the established order of things." Tecumseh later would be killed in battle in the War of 1812. Before he died, he summarized his vision of how to be a man this way:

1. Live your life that the fear of death can never enter your heart.
2. Trouble no one about his religion.
3. Respect others in their views and demand that they respect yours.
4. Love your life, perfect your life, beautify all things in your life. Seek to make your life long and of service to your people.
5. Prepare a noble death song for the day when you go over the great divide.
6. Always give a word or sign of salute when meeting or passing a friend, or even a stranger, if in a lonely place.
7. Show respect to all people, but grovel to none.
8. When you rise in the morning, give thanks for the light, for your life, for your strength. Give thanks for your food and for the joy of living. If you see no reason to give thanks, the fault lies in yourself.
9. Abuse no one and no thing, for abuse turns the wise ones to fools and robs the spirit of its vision.
10. When your time comes to die, be not like those whose hearts are filled with fear of death, so that when their time comes they weep and pray for a little more time to live their lives over again in a different way. Sing your death song, and die like a hero going home.[1]

---

[1] Joel Diederik Beversluis, *Sourcebook of the World's Religions*, New World Library, 2000.

New York Fire Department Code of Conduct

SERVICE: The Department continues its unwavering call to protect and serve.

BRAVERY: Bravery is the ability to overcome fear through fortitude, instinct, compassion for others and training.

SAFETY: We strive to keep our citizens free from danger, especially deliberate, harmful acts. With the best equipment and training, the Department can reduce the risk to the public and its members at fires, emergencies and medical incidents.

HONOR: The enormous commitment necessary to perform the Department's tasks requires excellence of character. We inspire each other through pride in our unit, which is a belief that every action reflects on all the members of the unit, both past and present.

DEDICATION: A commitment to the objectives of our mission is an essential part of our code of conduct. The faithful observance of duty calls for us to fulfill our obligations professionally and honestly.

PREPAREDNESS: By combining all of the components of our core values, the FDNY will maintain its constant state of readiness to meet all threats and challenges, traditional and new.

Miyamoto Musashi's 21 Steps to Self-Reliance

Miyamoto Musashi was a samurai in seventeenth-century Japan who remained undefeated in more than sixty individual matches. He wrote *The Book of Five Rings* late in his life to explain his Zen philosophy on how a man should live. His final act was to write "The Way of Walking Alone," which makes up these twenty-one rules on living as a man.

1. Do not turn your back on the various Ways of this world.
2. Do not scheme for physical pleasure.
3. Do not intend to rely on anything.
4. Consider yourself lightly; consider the world deeply.
5. Do not ever think in acquisitive terms.
6. Do not regret things about your own personal life.
7. Do not envy another's good or evil.
8. Do not lament parting on any road whatsoever.
9. Do not complain or feel bitterly about yourself or others.
10. Have no heart for approaching the path of love.
11. Do not have preferences.
12. Do not harbor hopes for your own personal home.
13. Do not have a liking for delicious food for yourself.
14. Do not carry antiques carried down from generation to generation.
15. Do not fast so that it affects you physically.
16. While it's different with military equipment, do not be fond of material things.
17. While on the Way, do not begrudge death.
18. Do not be intent on possessing valuables for a fief in old age.
19. Respect the Gods and Buddhas, but do not depend on them.
20. Though you give up your life, do not give up your honor.
21. Never depart from the Way of the Martial Arts.

Texas Ranger Code of Conduct

To advance the objective of the department in preserving order and protecting the lives, rights, privileges, and property of the people in the State of Texas to the best of my ability and in an entirely impartial manner.

To practice at all times the motto of this organization: "Courtesy, Service, Protection."

To keep myself clean and presentable, and in good physical, mental, and moral health.

To know and obey orders and instructions at all times.

To keep all state equipment entrusted to me fully accounted for and in proper condition.

To qualify as a voter, and to vote my convictions as a citizen on all public questions and political races, but to take no other part in any public politics or campaigns.

To conduct my business in a straightforward manner, relying upon poise, competence, and discretion rather than threats and argument to carry out my duties.

To take up matters affecting me and my position with my immediate superior and through proper channels.

To submit through proper channels constructive suggestions for the betterment of the department and its service.

To conduct myself at all times, both on and off duty, in such a gentlemanly manner that I may merit the voluntary commendation of all law-abiding citizens and visitors with whom I come in contact, both those with whom I meet in carrying out my duties and those I shall live among as a citizen in order that credit may be reflected upon the Texas Department of Public Safety.

The US Marine Corps' Creed

ARTICLE I: I am an American, fighting in the forces which guard my country and our way of life. I am prepared to give my life in their defense.

ARTICLE II: I will never surrender of my own free will. If in command, I will never surrender the members of my command while they still have the means to resist.

ARTICLE III: If I am captured I will continue to resist by all means available. I will make every effort to escape and to aid others to escape. I will accept neither parole nor special favors from the enemy.

ARTICLE IV: If I become a prisoner of war, I will keep faith with my fellow prisoners. I will give no information nor take part in any action which might be harmful to my comrades. If I am senior, I will take command. If not, I will obey lawful orders of those appointed over me and will back them in every way.

ARTICLE V: When questioned, should I become a prisoner of war, I am required to give name, rank, service number, and date of birth. I will evade answering further questions to the utmost of my ability. I will make no oral or written statements disloyal to my country or its allies or harmful to their cause.

ARTICLE VI: I will never forget that I am an American, fighting for freedom, responsible for my actions, and dedicated to the principles which made my country free. I will trust in my God and in the United States of America.

The Seven Virtues of Bushidō

The Japanese code of Bushidō, which translates to the "way of the warrior," is the code of moral principles that samurai were required to follow. During the Tokugawa Shogunate (1603–1868), the seven rules of Bushidō were formalized into Japanese feudal law.

1. Yuki (Courage): A Samurai must possess the bravery/ courage to face all of life's challenges with a strong and moral heart.
2. Jin (Benevolence): This is a magnanimous and compassionate state of mind that embraces the idea that all people are fundamentally the same and should be treated with the same respect regardless of station or situation.
3. Rei (Etiquette): A Samurai must respect himself and others by being a gentleman.
4. Makoto (Honesty): Honesty and integrity must be sought at all times.
5. Chugi (Loyalty): Duty to family and country is a fundamental aspect of this virtue.
6. Gi (Rectitude): Gi is a rightness of principle or practice, exact conformity to truth, integrity, honesty, and justice.
7. Meiyo (Honor): Meiyo is the sum of the previous six virtues, as someone who practices the code of Bushido would certainly be honorable.

Pirate Code of Conduct

Even pirates lived by codes of honor, as without them even they would perish. The Pirate Code of Conduct listed in Bartholomew Roberts's shipboard articles in 1721 was severe. It's a fun code, but it breaks the Golden Rule.

1. Every man shall have an equal vote in affairs of moment. He shall have an equal title to the fresh provisions or strong liquors at any time seized, and shall use them at pleasure unless a scarcity may make it necessary for the common good that a retrenchment may be voted.

2. Every man shall be called fairly in turn by the list on board of prizes, because over and above their proper share, they are allowed a shift of clothes. But if they defraud the company to the value of even one dollar in plate, jewels, or money, they shall be marooned. If any man rob another he shall have his nose and ears slit, and be put ashore where he shall be sure to encounter hardships.

3. None shall game for money either with dice or cards.

4. The lights and candles should be put out at eight at night, and if any of the crew desire to drink after that hour they shall sit upon the open deck without lights.

5. Each man shall keep his piece, cutlass, and pistols at all times clean and ready for action.

6. No boy or woman to be allowed amongst them. If any man shall be found seducing any of the latter sex and carrying her to sea in disguise he shall suffer death.

7. He that shall desert the ship or his quarters in time of battle shall be punished by death or marooning.

8. None shall strike another on board the ship, but every man's quarrel shall be ended on shore by sword or pistol in this manner. At the word of command from the quartermaster, each man being previously placed back to back, shall turn and fire immediately. If any man do not, the quartermaster shall knock the piece out of his hand. If both miss their aim they shall take to their cutlasses, and he that draweth first blood shall be declared the victor.

9. No man shall talk of breaking up their way of living till each has a share of 1,000. Every man who shall become a cripple or lose a limb in the service shall have 800 pieces of eight from the common stock and for lesser hurts proportionately.

10. The captain and the quartermaster shall each receive two shares of a prize, the master gunner and boatswain, one and one half shares, all other officers one and one quarter, and private gentlemen of fortune one share each.

11. The musicians shall have rest on the Sabbath Day only by right. On all other days by favor only.

Gene Autry's Cowboy Code of Honor

1. A cowboy never takes unfair advantage—even of an enemy.
2. A cowboy never betrays a trust. He never goes back on his word.
3. A cowboy always tells the truth.
4. A cowboy is kind and gentle to small children, old folks, and animals.
5. A cowboy is free from racial and religious intolerances.

6. A cowboy is always helpful when someone is in trouble.
7. A cowboy is always a good worker.
8. A cowboy respects womanhood, his parents, and his nation's laws.
9. A cowboy is clean about his person in thought, word, and deed.
10. A cowboy is a patriot.

Hopalong Cassidy's Creed for American Boys and Girls

1. The highest badge of honor a person can wear is honesty. Be truthful at all times.
2. Your parents are the best friends you have. Listen to them and obey their instructions.
3. If you want to be respected, you must respect others. Show good manners in every way.
4. Only through hard work and study can you succeed. Don't be lazy.
5. Your good deeds always come to light. So don't boast or be a show-off.
6. If you waste time or money today, you will regret it tomorrow. Practice thrift in all ways.
7. Many animals are good and loyal companions. Be friendly and kind to them.
8. A strong, healthy body is a precious gift. Be neat and clean.
9. Our country's laws are made for your protection. Observe them carefully.
10. Children in many foreign lands are less fortunate than you. Be glad and proud you are an American.

Wild Bill Hickock's Deputy Marshal's Code of Conduct

1. I will be brave, but never careless.
2. I will obey my parents. They DO know best.
3. I will be neat and clean at all times.
4. I will be polite and courteous.
5. I will protect the weak and help them.
6. I will study hard.
7. I will be kind to animals and care for them.
8. I will respect my flag and my country.
9. I will attend my place of worship regularly.

The Lone Ranger Creed

1. I believe that to have a friend, a man must be one.
2. That all men are created equal and that everyone has within himself the power to make this a better world.
3. That God put the firewood there, but that every man must gather and light it himself.
4. In being prepared physically, mentally, and morally to fight when necessary for that which is right.
5. That a man should make the most of what equipment he has.
6. That "this government, of the people, by the people, and for the people," shall live always.
7. That men should live by the rule of what is best for the greatest number.
8. That sooner or later . . . somewhere . . . somehow . . . we must settle with the world and make payment for what we have taken.

9. That all things change, but the truth, and the truth alone lives on forever.
10. I believe in my Creator, my country, my fellow man.

Roy Rogers Riders Club Rules

1. Be neat and clean.
2. Be courteous and polite.
3. Always obey your parents.
4. Protect the weak and help them.
5. Be brave, but never take chances.
6. Study hard and learn all you can.
7. Be kind to animals and care for them.
8. Eat all your food and never waste any.
9. Love God and go to Sunday School regularly.
10. Always respect our flag and our country.

US Navy Sailor's Creed

1. I am a United States Sailor.
2. I will support and defend the Constitution of the United States of America and I will obey the orders of those appointed over me.
3. I represent the fighting spirit of the Navy and those who have gone before me to defend freedom and democracy around the world.
4. I proudly serve my country's Navy combat team with Honor, Courage and Commitment.
5. I am committed to excellence and the fair treatment of all.

US Navy SEAL Code of Honor

1. In times of war or uncertainty there is a special breed of warrior ready to answer our Nation's call; a common man with an uncommon desire to succeed. Forged by adversity, he stands alongside America's finest special operations forces to serve his country and the American people, and to protect their way of life. I am that man.

2. My Trident is a symbol of honor and heritage. Bestowed upon me by the heroes who have gone before, it embodies the trust of those whom I have sworn to protect. By wearing the Trident, I accept the responsibility of my chosen profession and way of life. It is a privilege that I must earn every day.

3. My loyalty to Country and Team is beyond reproach. I humbly serve as a guardian to my fellow Americans, always ready to defend those who are unable to defend themselves. I do not advertise the nature of my work, nor seek recognition for my actions. I voluntarily accept the inherent hazards of my profession, placing the welfare and security of others before my own.

4. I serve with honor on and off the battlefield. The ability to control my emotions and my actions, regardless of circumstance, sets me apart from other men. Uncompromising integrity is my standard. My character and honor are steadfast. My word is my bond.

5. We expect to lead and be led. In the absence of orders I will take charge, lead my teammates, and accomplish the mission. I lead by example in all situations.

6. I will never quit. I persevere and thrive on adversity. My Nation expects me to be physically harder and mentally stronger than my enemies. If knocked down, I will get back up, every time. I will draw on every remaining ounce of strength to protect my teammates and to accomplish the mission. I am never out of the fight.

7. We demand discipline. We expect innovation. The lives of my teammates and the success of the mission depend on me—my technical skill, tactical proficiency, and attention to detail. My training is never complete.

8. We train for war and fight to win. I stand ready to bring the full spectrum of combat power to bear in order to achieve my mission and the goals established by my country. The execution of my duties will be swift and violent when required, yet guided by the very principles I serve to defend.

9. Brave men have fought and died building the proud tradition and feared reputation that I am bound to uphold. In the worst of conditions, the legacy of my teammates steadies my resolve and silently guides my every deed. I will not fail.

About the Author

FRANK MINITER IS A *New York Times* best-selling author and investigative journalist with a penchant for outdoor adventure. He has fly-fished everywhere from the Amazon's Xingu River to Scotland's River Spey to Japan's freestone streams. He has hunted everything from Russian bear in Kaleria to elk with the Apache to kudu in the Kalahari. Along the way, he was taught to box by Floyd Patterson, graduated from the oldest private military college (Norwich University) in the US, and has, again and again, gotten into the street to run with Spanish fighting bulls in Pamplona's San Fermín festival.

Miniter's other books include *The Ultimate Man's Survival Guide: Recovering the Lost Art of Manhood, The Future of the Gun, Saving the Bill of Rights,* and *The Politically Incorrect Guide to Hunting.* Miniter is a *Forbes* contributor, a contributing writer for *Outdoor Life* magazine, and a field editor for *American Hunter* magazine. He has written for *Boys' Life, National Review,* the *Washington Times,* the *Washington Examiner,* and many other publications. He is often a guest on national radio and television shows. You can find him at FrankMiniter.com.